Praise for *Keys to Perception*

"Buy all of Ivo's books. Study them. D
return and study them some more."

—**T. Thorn Coyle,** author of *Kissing the Limitless: Deep Magic and the Great Work of Transforming Yourself and the World*

"*Keys to Perception* is another masterful work by Ivo Dominguez Jr., artfully blending deep metaphysical insight into the nature of psychic perception with clear and direct instructions and examples. Only someone with a long history of direct experience and an educated understanding of the phenomenon could write this book to both convey useful skills to beginners and provide new perspectives for seasoned psychics. Grounded and practical as well as flexible in approach. I look forward to recommending this to students, friends, and peers alike."

—**Christopher Penczak,** award-winning author and co-founder of the Temple of Witchcraft

"For some people, witchcraft is about herbs and candles and prayers to the gods. For some others, magic is about the proper grimoire and ritual protocols. *Keys to Perception* is for those who want to *see* and *feel* and *know directly.* Once you can do this, magic is forever transformed. Developing this perception takes work. Even those who are naturally psychic can greatly improve their accuracy and power through training. Ivo presents a battery of methods that will give you the skills to see and communicate with a whole other world, leaving no doubt about the realities of magic."

—**Jason Miller,** author of *Financial Sorcery* and *The Sorcerer's Secrets,* and creator of The Strategic Sorcery Course

"Written as only one who possesses great knowledge and experience can do, *Keys to Perception* is sure to be a classic 'must read' in the field of psychic development. This may well be the most practical and useful book on the subject I've read to date."

—**Raven Grimassi,** author of *Communing with the Ancestors*

"Ivo Dominguez Jr. has demystified the mystical without compromising its beauty. He invites you into his process and shows the ways for readers to make it all their own. Part workbook, part testimony to the great Mysteries, *Keys to Perception* is an absolutely essential guide for magick practitioners of all levels."

—**Courtney Weber,** author of *Tarot for One*

"Having spent fifty of my eighty-eight years, reading, writing, and actively taking part in all areas of the paranormal, I feel qualified to say to my students in all honesty, 'I wish I had had this book when I was twenty.'

"Over the years that I have known and worked with Ivo, there has never been a time when I have not learned something from him. Despite the gap in our ages and the very few differences of opinion, he has always been able to open my eyes to something I've missed. Now, with his latest book (and, I think, his best) he has put before his readers what amounts to a complete course on the Magical Arts. As always, his style is clear, concise, and delivered without frills or irrelevancies. He writes with the authority coming from years of personal experience, tempered by the ability to know when to change, adapt, and take new and often uncharted directions.

"Chapters two to seven are good, solid, basic information for those new to this way of thinking. Ivo pulls no punches—building a foundation is hard work and needs dedication and patience. Eight, nine, and ten take you much deeper but make sure you feel on safe ground. Eleven to sixteen will provide you with what can amount to a lifetime of refining what has gone before. In short, Ivo has placed before his readers *his life work on himself.* Here is all he has learned, discovered, practiced, and, I suspect, at times has despaired over, and now offers to those who come after him. Whether you have some experience or are a complete newcomer, *Keys to Perception* is a book to have close by. It will certainly be on my shelves. Ivo has written many books and I am sure will go on to write more, but this is one to keep on the shelves and refer to again and again. I will certainly add it to the recommended reading list for SOL (Servants of the Light) students."

—**Dolores Ashcroft-Nowicki,** Director of Studies, SOL

KEYS TO Perception

A Practical Guide to Psychic Development

IVO DOMINGUEZ JR.

WEISER BOOKS

This edition first published in 2017 by
Weiser Books, an imprint of
Red Wheel/Weiser, LLC
With offices at:
65 Parker Street, Suite 7
Newburyport, MA 01950
www.redwheelweiser.com

ISBN: 978-1-57863-620-4

Library of Congress Cataloging-in-Publication Data
available upon request

Cover design by Jim Warner
Cover images © Shutterstock
Interior by Howie Severson
Typeset in Warnock Pro

Printed in Canada
MAR
10 9 8 7 6 5 4 3 2 1

This book is dedicated to my beloved James Conrad Welch, to James Eric Dickinson, Michael Glen Smith, and to all my kith and kin in the Assembly of the Sacred Wheel. A special thanks to my grandmother Zenaida, who was the first person to affirm my visions.

Contents

Prelude

Why do you want to open or improve your psychic senses? The answer to that question actually can have a significant impact on what is possible for you. The inner senses, the psychic senses, and your use of them are mediated by your thoughts, emotions, motivations, intentions, and more. Taking time to do a self-assessment of your reasons for wanting to be more psychic will help you move more quickly in your development, as you will know more about your obstacles before you begin. I suggest that you actually do so as the first exercise in this book. As you proceed through this book, and after you finish it, you may wish to revisit the question once more.

I've encountered many people who have told me that they used to be much more open psychically and that at some point something closed them down. Often, it is suggested that fear or social conditioning has much to do with this diminishment of perception. This notion is certainly true in the sense that we live in a culture that, for the most part, is not welcoming and, in fact, often ridicules those who claim to perceive something beyond physical reality. Sometimes certain types of religious experiences are granted an exception, and sometimes not. There is in my estimation another common set of emotional reactions that will shut down psychic perception. The crisper and more reliable your psychic perceptions become, the more accountable you are for how you use that information and guidance. This is not merely a fear of power, but of how and when you will use it, and how it will change your relationship to your life and the people and things in it. The better that you know yourself, your values, and the direction of your moral compass, the more courage you will have. Remember that courage is the power to act in the presence of fear.

There are also those whose psychic senses have been throttled down because these people are overwhelmed by the experience of having their powers open. I share several techniques in this book that will give you control over your inner senses. It may also be that you have been tormented by having received information of a negative sort and you had no capacity to change the outcomes. In both that case and in the situation of being overwhelmed, I suggest a simple affirmation, prayer, or dialogue with yourself to be done ideally once a day when you rise or before you go to sleep. You may adjust the wording for whatever makes sense for you, but the gist of it should be something like this:

> *"Let me know those things where I can make a change, warn others, or be better prepared, and spare me from all others."*

There have been times in my life when I repeated this line daily for weeks, and then gaps of years before I needed it once more.

In my experience, all living things have psychic capabilities. Although to some degree, talent and potential do matter, the utility of your psychic senses is more a matter of practice and application. And by practice, I mean *practice*; the regular use of your psychic senses is the surest way to making them reliable and useful. When possible, find people who are interested in developing their psychism so that you can share encouragement and feedback with each other.

Before turning the page and beginning the main body of the book, I'd like you to recall a moment of wonder that you've had in experiencing the world beyond the physical senses. Pay attention whenever you marvel at something or feel awe. Wonder will feed the growth of your psychic skills and is an antidote for naysayers within and without.

CHAPTER 1

Opening the Inner Senses

Clearing and Brightening the Mind

How well and how crisply you perceive the world can vary dramatically. Most often, you notice this variation only when you are at one of the highs or lows of perceptual acuity. Sometimes the colors of a flower that you have seen before become especially vivid and nuanced. Other times, when you are listening to a favorite piece of music, you can distinguish the role of every instrument and hear the slightest tremble of emotion in a voice. There are also times when, although the external reality is almost the same, your perception seems wrapped in fog and cotton. In part, this is a result of your emotional state of being, but that is not the only or even the primary determinant.

The clarity and strength of your perceptions are strongly regulated by the amount of attention, or the proportion of your mind's power that is allocated to your attention. This allocation of mental resources is often unconscious, but it can be done with conscious effort as well. When you focus in on a single voice in a crowded room or look closely enough at an apple to see the specks and streaks of color on its skin, your attention shifts the balance of your mental resources and thus your strength of perception. This variability in sensory and perceptual sharpness also applies to your inner senses, although this is not as apparent. Since the inner senses are decoded and interpreted through your physical senses, efforts to focus more of your mental processes on sharpening the physical senses also refine the inner senses. Perception occurs in the mind, and by clearing and brightening the mind, we open more fully to our inner senses. What follows is a sampling of methods that reliably help prepare you for making better use of your inner senses.

Meditation

The suggestion that you make meditation a part of your regular practice is very popular in most magickal and spiritual teachings and traditions. In part, the reason is that meditation supports self-knowledge and encourages spiritual development. Meditation also helps clear and brighten the mind so that you become more aware of your inner senses. In the context of opening the inner senses, my working definition for meditation is the art of changing waking consciousness into a higher active state of being with the goal of expanding our capacity to remain in that state. Although it can start with relaxation or produce relaxation as one of the results, that is not the goal of meditation. Meditation is not intended to be sedation; it is how you exercise and condition the Self.

I have encountered many people who say that they've tried to meditate and that they just can't do it. Their most common complaint is that they can't quiet their mind. Have you ever seen a person in the middle of a bout of hard crying or had one yourself? It is neither easy nor useful to try to stop the crying until it runs its course. For many people, when they try to make meditation a part of their practice, every stray thought and feeling that they have held back pours forth. This is not a sign of failure in meditation; it means that the meditation is working and is a part of the cleansing and purification that come with the work. Others find fault with their attempts because they can't meditate very long or deeply. Meditation is a form of exercise; as such, it is reasonable to have the expectation that your beginning efforts will be short and of low intensity and that over time you will become more capable of duration and depth.

- If you have a hard time sitting still, then try to meditate while standing or walking; alternatively, look into forms of moving meditation such as tai chi, qigong, kinhin, or labyrinth walking.
- If you are worried about falling asleep, don't worry; it happens to everyone sooner or later.

If you are always falling asleep during meditation while seated, try placing your fist against your chin so as to prop up your head for just a moment. Then move your fist away and keep your forearm perpendicular to the table or chair arm. Should you begin to get drowsy, your arm will drop and rouse you. You can do roughly the same thing while lying down, so long as your elbow is supported.

There are many types of meditation, and I encourage you to seek out books, groups, and online instructions. Two of the major branches of meditation are *open* and *focused* meditation:

- Open meditation often starts with attention on your breathing, then with a focus on your thoughts and feelings, without judgment, with the goal of being without doing in order to clear away the chatter we normally call thoughts. The aspiration is to become like a transparent, still ball of awareness that senses the whole universe.

- Focused meditation starts in a similar way, but focuses on an idea, a phrase, a symbol to more deeply understand it, or a single external focus such as a candle flame or a simple drum beat.

The intention of the repetition or fixation is not to zone out. It is not the same as a trance, which is a more passive state in which you prepare yourself for receptivity. Also, do not confuse pathworkings or visualizations with meditation. These tend to be tools for teaching, healing, and so on, and the focus is on their content and a process with a specific purpose rather than the refinement of the mind as a primary goal.

Warming Up

Whether it is physical or psychic exertion, warming up to prepare yourself for the effort is a good idea. Often people skip over this step due to impatience, a feeling of being rushed, or the urgency of a situation. My answer to that reluctance is that there are swift and simple ways to prepare for inner work that can be learned and executed quickly. The two methods I share here can be used individually or together. In both cases, a physical action is performed. Some warm-ups use only visualization, but the more levels and parts of the Self you involve, the more the inner senses will be integrated into your awareness.

IAO

The intoning of IAO (*Eeee-Ahhh-Ohhh*) is used for a wide range of magickal and spiritual purposes. Intoning IAO is an effective and simple technique to awaken your psychism, your inner senses. Before we see how to use it in opening the inner senses, let's look into its meaning and history. IAO has been said to mean numerous things depending on which practitioner is asked.

- Esoteric Christians would tell you that IAO is one of the ways that the early Gnostic Christians intoned the name of God.
- IAO is also associated with the gods Hermes and Iacchus, and is also the name of a Phoenician god of light.
- In various streams of Ceremonial Magick, IAO is understood as a formula or an acronym, as, for instance, for the names Isis, Apophis, and Osiris, and thus represents creation, destruction, and restoration.
- IAO may be understood to be *I* as the God, *A* as the Divine Child, and *O* as the Goddess.
- I have also heard it described as representing the three pillars of the Tree of Life with *I* being force, *A* being synthesis, and *O* being form.

It may be all these things and more, but I think that these are associations and descriptions to connect the IAO to a specific system, rather than being inherent properties of IAO in themselves. My perspective is that it is from the vowel sounds themselves that the power arises. To be able to intone IAO (*Eeee-Ahhh-Ohhh*), the mouth, the tongue, and breath move through the three positions from which all other vowel sounds arise. When someone intones the IAO, the focus of the physical sensation of vibration moves from the head to the throat to the chest. I believe that what is being activated is deeply rooted in both our neurology and subtle bodies. In the same way that intoning AUM moves energy and modifies consciousness, so does intoning IAO, but with a different assortment of changes in energy and consciousness.

Before doing exercises, rituals, divination, or any activity that uses the inner senses, take three deep breaths to prepare yourself, and then intone IAO three to five times. When you breathe to prepare yourself, and during the toning, breathe from the belly. Many people tend to breathe from the chest, perhaps from habit or because of a concern that their belly will look bigger if they breathe from their diaphragm. Belly breathing is better for this technique as well as many others. The duration of each vowel sound should be one full breath. Aim for a clear, resonant tone that is loud enough so that you can feel it in your body. When possible, do this while standing, and if that is not possible, then lift your chin slightly as you tone.

It is important that you follow the pattern of IAO. In other words, sound out *Eeee,* then *Ahhh,* then *Ohhh* and count that as one repetition. I have observed people sound out the *Eeee* several times and then move on to repeating the *Ahhh* several times, but this technique does not have as strong an effect. Focus on how the energy descends from the top of your head and fills your body. Pay attention to the sound, your breath, and your sensations to maximize the impact of the IAO toning. When you are done toning, take three deep breaths and proceed with your work.

Four-Fold Breathing

> *The mind is the king of the senses, and the breath is the king of the mind.*
>
> —Hatha Yoga Pradipika

Four-Fold Breathing, also known as Square Breathing or *Samavritti,* as is presented here, is a simplified version from

Pranayama Yoga. Breathing is both an involuntary and a voluntary process, and as such is both a threshold and a bridge between different levels of consciousness. When you focus on breathing, you are also focusing on your body, the flow of life energy, your awareness, and more. Four-Fold Breathing recognizes breath as having four phases: inhaling, lungs full, exhaling, and lungs empty. The goal is to make each of these four phases of breathing of equal duration.

When you engage in Four-Fold Breathing, the various rhythms in the body such as the heartbeat, breath, and the pulse of cerebrospinal fluid fall into alignment with the movement of energy in your aura. The result is a greater sense of calm and a greater sense of alertness. If symbolic connections make it easier for you to invest yourself in the process, then think of Four-Fold Breathing as representing natural cycles such as sunrise, noon, sunset, and midnight. Other possible correlations include cycles of the moon—first quarter, full, last quarter, and dark—or any other four-station patterns.

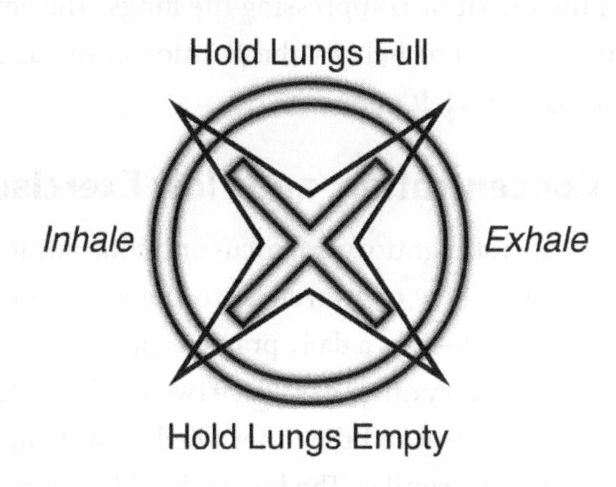

Four-Fold Breathing

To engage in Four-Fold Breathing, you count to keep time for each of the four phases. Try a count of four or five in your first efforts. Depending on your lung capacity and how fast you count, you will need to adjust the number higher or lower. When your lungs are empty or full, you hold your breath for the same length of time as the inhalation and the exhalation. Ideally, continue with your counted breathing for one or two minutes before proceeding with the work at hand. If you are short on time, complete at least four cycles of Four-Fold Breathing. When you hold your breath, hold it with your belly, not your throat. Once again, for magickal and spiritual purposes, please use your diaphragm to manage your breathing. When you hold your breath in Four-Fold Breathing, your throat should feel relaxed. Be gentle and careful with yourself if you have asthma, high blood pressure, are late in pregnancy, or have any other condition that may have an impact on your breathing and blood pressure. In general, if there are difficulties, they arise during the lungs full or empty phases as a result of holding them by clenching the throat or compressing the lungs. The empty and the full lungs should be held by the position of the diaphragm, and the air passages left open.

Focus, Concentration, and Flow Exercises

Let's begin with a straightforward focus and concentration exercise before adding flow of awareness to the work. Ideally, this exercise should be done as a daily practice, but at the very least, it should be done every other day. Place two small bowls in front of you, with one empty and the other filled with small pebbles, beans, or something similar. The bowls should be easy to reach so that you can pick up the pebbles. Select a target thought that you will hold during this task. The target thought can be an internally generated image such as a triangle, a circle and dot, and so on. It can also be an external image such as a candle flame, the point of a crystal, or some other simple object. Regardless of whether this target thought is visualized or observed, it should be relatively plain to minimize the potential for distraction. Set a timer (an egg timer or your phone, for example) for five minutes. Take a breath and clear your mind; then focus on only the target thought. Every time that your thoughts stray, take a pebble and place it in the empty bowl. When the timer goes off, count the number of times your thoughts wandered.

For the first week, keep the timer at five minutes. At the beginning of the second week, increase it to seven minutes. As the number of pebbles drops with more practice, consider lengthening the duration of the exercise. Try not to get preoccupied with the number of pebbles after each session. Look for the trend of improvement and be aware that some days you will do better than others.

Focused Flow

Studies conducted at world-renowned museums such as the Metropolitan Museum of Art and the Louvre have shown that the average length of time visitors spend gazing at each piece is somewhere in the range of fifteen to seventeen seconds. As a response to this, there is a *slow art* movement that encourages people to spend longer periods of time with individual pieces of art, rather than flitting from piece to piece. Having experienced this slow approach, I have discovered that it is very helpful in developing focus, concentration, and flow in awareness, which heightens the inner senses.

This exercise involves looking at one piece of art for fifteen minutes. It would be lovely if you would do this at a museum, but you can do it at home with a print as well. The first time you do this exercise, use a piece that you have not already studied at length. If you choose to use an image found online, please print it out because the distractions provided by the objects and associations near your screen are not compatible with the exercise. Place the print against a blank wall or table so that it is the primary visual stimulation in your field of sight. Make sure that your phone's ringer is turned off and other sources of interruption are minimized. Arrange yourself in a position so that you will be comfortable for at least fifteen minutes. Set a timer for fifteen minutes, but place it so that you will not be able to glance at it and thus disrupt the exercise. If your physical sight is significantly impaired, you can adapt this exercise, using an intricate piece of fiber art, a quilt, embroidery, or a deeply textured oriental rug, for example. A complicated piece of music that you can repeat and pause will also work well.

Now start contemplating the art, by identifying the features that draw the focus of your eyes. Then look at the features again and focus on each one until you can distinguish each detail of line, color, texture, tonality, and so on in sharp detail. Begin again and spend time concentrating on each feature, trying to understand what is being communicated, what it signifies, how and why the artist chose to express in this specific way, and so on. Then start again with focusing on the features; you may also discover ones that had gone unnoticed. This pattern of focusing and concentrating will probably take longer each time it is repeated. After you believe that you have extracted all you can by focusing and concentrating, let your eyes move over the art and find the motion, the rhythm, the currents of interest that conduct your gaze. You can start with the order that you first noticed when you picked out the important features, and then allow yourself to follow little eddies and swirls of interest. Let your gaze and attention follow the movement and circulation in the art at different speeds because some things become apparent only when viewed at the right speed. Make note of any patterns or repetitions of elements that you see. After a time, stop and look at the piece in its entirety with a soft, unfocused gaze and see what insights and reactions arise within you. Repeat your flow observations and soft gaze contemplation until the timer goes off or you reach the limit of endurance, whichever comes first. Ideally, you should then write down an account of your impressions.

Part of the value of this exercise is that it builds the length and quality of your attention span. It also helps teach you what it feels like to let a fuller understanding of your perceptions to be built up slowly and cumulatively. Current norms and old biological programming tend to emphasize and condition you to make snap judgments and cursory evaluations. Psychic perception is multilayered, and the first impression rarely tells the whole story. Indeed, often the first layer is too ambiguous or just enough to confuse you. I have had many students come to the conclusion that they had scant talents in the psychic arts because their perceptions didn't all come in a flash. Although at some times and for some people, clear and detailed psychic perceptions are quick and unequivocal, this is the exception rather than the norm. Even those in the exceptional category would benefit from slowing down and letting the information unfold and reveal more context. The progression of psychic perception can be likened to a large image downloading on a slow Internet connection. It may appear all at once but be fuzzy and filled with distortions, or it may appear in slowly refreshing strips that become clearer with each pass. If you move on when you have just begun making some sense of the image, you may miss important details. Another comparison would be that of a video that pauses or repeats as it buffers during a download. It may be that you will see more of the message if you wait for all of it to arrive in your conscious awareness.

Perhaps contemplating art for fifteen minutes may seem grueling at first, but like most exercises, it gets easier with repetition. The pattern of focus, concentration, and flow used in appreciating the art is extremely useful in psychic work as well. After you have worked with the slow art exercise, apply a similar pattern to your efforts in psychic perception. When you are in the focus part of the cycle, the objective is to collect as many details as possible from each component of your psychic impressions. Do not censor, repress, or rule out anything. Just observe and attend to your inner senses. In the concentration part of the cycle, try to derive meaning from your observations. Ask yourself if what you perceive is representational, symbolic, or a combination of the two. Following the period of concentration and contemplation, dig back in with more focused observations. It is common for more to become discernable because the concentration cycle helps tune in, or dial in, your inner senses. When you feel you have repeated the focus and concentration cycles enough, move on to the flow that connects all the components. Move through the flow of components and ideas in more than one direction. Seek out the relationships between sets of components and ideas, not just pairs in sequence. Finally, move to a state of inner stillness and allow for a comprehension of the whole to emerge.

Opening the Inner Sight

For many people, the inner sight—seeing spirits, auras, and visions—is the holy grail of psychic development. I will share some methods for opening and improving the inner eye, the

Third Eye, that work for most people. Even so, not everyone will develop 20/20 psychic sight quickly or perhaps ever. This is not an obstacle to being an effective practitioner, but being overly critical of whatever unique combination of abilities you possess is a major obstacle. Work on all the inner senses because they all can be improved, and embrace what you have and maximize your strengths, whatever they may be.

Psychic sight comes in many forms and variations. In this book, I'll touch on three major categories. For example, sometimes the inner sight is overlain on top of physical sight and is directed by where the physical eyes focus; this is the first category. For some people, a soft, unfocused gaze is more effective when using the inner sight with the eyes open. With your eyes open, the inner sight can range from barely visible or almost transparent to so bright and colorful that it obscures the physical world.

There is also a variant of psychic sight with open eyes that is not an overlay and temporarily changes the appearance of something in a way that looks completely solid and physical. This variation can be as subtle as a bush at the side of the road looking like an animal for a moment as you pass it, or as jarring as changing your stride to avoid bumping into someone who isn't there an instant later. Psychic sight with the physical eyes shut and the visions seen within the mind is altogether another category. These inward visions can also run the full gamut from flashes of color and simple shapes to full and detailed panoramas. They can be like still images, slide shows, or movies projected behind your eyelids. These inward visions may refer to or have linkages to your physical surroundings, or they may refer to other places, planes of being, or time frames.

In the third category of psychic sight, the inner visions are intentionally projected onto external objects. When you look into a crystal ball, a black mirror, or a flame to seek visions, you are using a physical stimulus as an anchor to gain greater control over the flow of images that normally occur with your eyes shut. When no specially prepared objects are available, you can get reasonably good results using a plain wall or large, blank sheet of paper. This practice of projecting your inner sight onto an external object is often called *skrying* (or *scrying*) and can bring the best or the worst of the qualities of the eyes-open and the inward-sight approaches to bear on your efforts. There is an entire chapter on skrying later in this book, but I recommend that you work through the chapters in order rather than leaping ahead.

Visual Fluidity Exercise

The mind constantly attempts to find recognizable patterns in the stream of sensory impressions. The mind extrapolates and fills in gaps as it tries to fit what it finds to something that is known. This way of thinking certainly is favored by evolution because finding the signal in the noise, such as seeing the predator or the cliff, quickly can lead to survival or death.

Sometimes this tendency to detect patterns can result in finding meaning or identifiable images or sounds that are *not* present. The general term for finding specific things in any kind of random stimulus is *apophenia*. The specific term for the mind perceiving images and sounds in random stimulus is *pareidolia*. Some skeptics argue that most psychism and divinatory systems are fueled by delusions born of apophenia to explain away the phenomena; the skeptics are half right. That said, it is the capacity to discern order and meaning from meager clues that is one of our most important mental gifts. This is why we can understand what a stick figure is or make sense of a quick sketch. I think it may also be what provided the psychological and neurological basis for the use of symbols, pictographs, and alphabets. Often our visual psychic sight is a faint signal that is drowned out in the stronger input of physical sight. We also have habits, conditioning, and learned contexts for our physical sight that take precedence in our normal state of consciousness. To counterbalance the primacy of physical sight, a greater fluidity of visual pattern seeking is needed.

When was the last time that you spent five to fifteen minutes looking at clouds and considering how many things you could see in them? This pleasant task encourages the sort of visual fluidity and imagination that opens the inner sight. You can also look at textured ceilings, walls, or any other broad expanse that has small details that can turn into a parade of scenes and images in the mind's eye. For the purpose of building visual fluidity, you'll do better with a larger field of view, so swirls in your coffee won't do.

Whenever possible, look at the sky for this exercise, because when you do so, your eyes shift their focus to their farthest range. In addition to relaxing the eyes, the far focus helps create an associative link to the task of seeing far with psychic sight. If you know that you are not likely to remember to do this exercise regularly, please add reminders in your calendar. The best results come when there is repetition every other day for three to five cloud-gazing sessions. After you make a concentrated effort, you can skip this practice for a few weeks before repeating it again. Most people experience more detail and clarity in their visual psychic impressions after only a few days of encouraging visual fluidity.

Gazing the Star

Physical sight requires adequate illumination. The physical eyes take in light that is either reflected or emitted by the objects that we see. The light that the physical eyes are capable of registering is a very small span of the frequencies on the electromagnetic spectrum. The inner eyes are capable of registering a much broader range of frequencies, including some that are not a part of the electromagnetic spectrum that I'll call subtle light. In truth, if we take into consideration that the universe is replete with the full range of the electromagnetic spectrum as well as all the subtle energies that lie beyond the physical, there are always ample sources of illumination. When the illumination is more than our eyes can cope with, it becomes a formless brilliance wherein we see nothing, or we clamp shut our metaphorical eyelids to block out the discomfort of too much light. This is one of the reasons that there is such a strong barrier to our normal waking conscious being given access to full psychic sight. The inner eyes, in addition to the functions that are the equivalent of those of the physical eyes, must also select the proper frequencies and focus not only in space but also in time and plane of reality.

The inner eyes, and for that matter the whole aura, can both receive and emit subtle light. The radiance that is given off by the subtle bodies is not only interlaced and interacting with the energies that surround it, but is also one of the means by which psychic sight is modulated. In ancient times, some people believed that rays that emanated from the eyes facilitated sight. This thinking, of course, was shown not to be true for the physical eyes, but, in a manner, it is true for the subtle eyes. The exercise I call *gazing the star* makes use of the capacity both to receive and to radiate subtle light to open and to calibrate psychic sight.

To begin the exercise, close your eyes and imagine that your entire body is filling with light so that you are glowing as if lit from within. Lift your chin slightly, and with your eyelids still shut, move your gaze upward to the top of the night sky that lives within you. Don't just imagine this motion; move your physical gaze upward as far as is comfortable. By the power of like calling to like, light to light, wish and will a star to ignite at the top of your inner heavens. By your light, call it forth. See the star grow brighter and brighter as you look at it. As it grows brighter, see rays of light burst forth from the star. The rays grow larger and longer until they reach down and touch you. The light of the star mingles with the light within you. Take a few deep breaths, and then take the light from above and the light from within and create a star upon your brow. Let the star upon your brow shine forth from your Third Eye.

Now open your physical eyes and proceed with whatever type of psychic visioning you wish to do. If you need to see more clearly with your inner senses, brighten the star upon your brow and send beams toward the object of your observation. In some cases, your aim is at something that you can focus your physical eyes on; in other cases, the beams you send forth have an aim guided by intention. Think of this as directing a spotlight drawn from your energy onto whatever needs to stand out against the background of all the other overlapping energies.

Third Eye Squint

I've needed glasses since high school; I was resistant to wearing them, so I learned the fine art of squinting. With each squint, I was able to read one more line on the blackboard until I could piece together the information. I eventually resigned myself to wearing glasses or contact lenses, but I still squint in the morning, before I don eye correction. Physical methods can often provide models for psychic methods. When something is just at the edge of your psychic sight's focus, make a brief, intense effort to see more. In essence, squint with your Third Eye. Most people can push beyond their normal level of psychic sight for short bursts with intensified concentration. With each squint of the Third Eye, you can collect more details that you can piece together. In general, the information you glean this way will be more accurate than straining for an extended period.

There are a few things that you may wish to try when using the *Third Eye squint*. Take in a breath as you focus your attention on the target and hold your breath with your diaphragm, not your throat. Exhale when you release your focus. Using your breathing this way helps create a stillness that improves seeing and limits the length of time that you will be exerting yourself. Before each repetition of the Third Eye squint, run through what you have gathered in the previous efforts so that you can direct your attention to new details rather than reworking what you have already seen. Be mindful of how you are feeling so that you can stop before you are too weary.

Parting the Veil

The method I call *parting the veil* for improving psychic sight works partly through its psychological impact and partly through magickal means. It is said that the physical world is a veil between us and the more expansive reality that surrounds us. Moreover, there are veils between each of the layers, the planes, of reality and perception. In many different systems of magickal practice, some version of a physical gesture is a figurative representation of the parting of these veils. The gesture acts as a message to the nonverbal parts of you, where most of your psychism dwells, that you are ready and interested in seeing beyond the physical realm. The gesture is also a way to direct energy to create a portal to see past the physical plane. Whether the veils thin to some degree or fully part is determined by how fully both the psychological and energetic aspects of the symbolic gesture are engaged.

To try this technique, begin by pressing your hands together in front of you. Your fingertips should be touching and pointed forward. You may do this with your eyes open or shut. Experiment to find out which is better for you. Using deep breaths that pull in energy from your surroundings, move energy from your core to your shoulders, down your arms, and into your hands. You may wish to push your hands together with a subtle pulsing pressure as the energy builds within and between them. When you intuit that you are ready, move your hands forward as if you were pushing your fingertips into the place where two curtains meet. Pull your hands apart using the same movement you would use to open the curtains, thus opening the veils and creating a portal for your sight. Stop running the energy in your hands; then look through the portal that you have opened.

It may be useful to repeat the parting of the veils gesture, either at the beginning or as an adjustment midway through your efforts at seeing. There is a modification to this technique that you may wish to try. After completing the steps described here, hold your hands close to your temples so that you narrow your field of view to the area of the portal. Continue to run energy through your hands if you are using this variant of the technique. Try different hand and finger positions to see how it modifies your perceptions.

Opening the Subtle Ears

The psychic equivalent of hearing is perhaps one of the most valuable and often unexplored of the inner senses. When we use our eyes, our sharpest focus is on a relatively small field of vision, and the range of color, tone, and texture is fairly limited. When we listen, our field of hearing encompasses the entirety of our surroundings. We don't hear just what our ears are pointed at, we hear in 360 degrees and in three dimensions. The amount of our brain that is set aside for processing sound is much greater than that which is used to process vision. This makes sense because the total range of sounds that we can discern is much larger than the range that we can see.

It also takes a considerable amount of neurological processing power to make sense of the variations in acoustics that allow us to know where things are, the size of the room, the texture of the floor, and many other characteristics by sound alone. When we listen to complicated sounds such as music with many instruments and voices, we have the ability to listen to it as a whole or to selectively increase our awareness of specific instruments or voices. It is something of a marvel the first time you realize that you can remix music in your mind. It is much harder to do something similar with your sight. Often, psychic impressions have many layers of information that are related to each other in a complicated web of relationships that each contribute to the meaning of the impression. Most of what we call psychic perception is the conversion of those impressions to an analogue of our physical senses. Hearing, in some regards, is much more nuanced than seeing and can decode some types of psychic impressions much more effectively.

To open the centers of psychic hearing, push some energy into your fingertips and gently rub the boney protuberance (mastoid process) behind each ear. Continue moving energy into these spots until you feel warmth, tingling, or some other indication that you have awakened the power in these centers. Then slowly move your hands away while visualizing cones of energy extending out from behind your ears. For a visual reference, you can imagine them to be like the speaker horns on an old Victrola record player. If that doesn't work with your sensibilities, try imagining two whirlpools of energy springing from behind your ears. Close your eyes and listen carefully to the physical sounds around you. You may be surprised to find that your physical hearing is sharper. Then extend your hearing and listen for the subtle sounds of any energies, spirits, thought forms, and so on that may be around you. Keep in mind that you can adjust the angle, size, and shape of the cones of energy that are augmenting your psychic hearing.

You may hear voices, though more often that is not the case. There is a strong cultural association with hearing voices and being mentally ill, which I believe inhibits the hearing of voices when you work to open the inner ears. If you do hear something that is similar to speaking or singing, that is wonderful. If you don't, it may come later as you continue to develop your psychic hearing.

It is more common to hear tones, percussive sounds, or something that resembles music. Sometimes it seems as if this exercise is not working, but if you pay close attention, you'll realize that it sounds as if the room that you are in has changed size or shape. One of the ways that psychic hearing manifests is in a sensing of the shape of how the multiple planes and veils of reality are interacting around you. It is also possible to sense the position and the motion of spirits around you. You may or may not identify it as hearing at first, but it arises from your psychic impressions being extrapolated into something understandable through the filters inherent to hearing.

Sometimes you will hear a snippet of something that continues to repeat. This could mean that some part of you does *not* believe that the information that is being offered has been understood. If a spirit is involved, then it may be repeating itself, until it has evidence that you have heard them. In either case, try to make sense of what you are hearing.

Should the meaning still elude you, imagine the same sounds in your mind as clearly and distinctly as you can, and then pause and listen again. This reiteration will signal that you are ready to hear more. After the pause, you may hear additional sounds that are a continuation of the message. Continue the process of repeating the sounds in your mind and pausing until the message is complete or as complete as it will be. The longer the segment that you capture, the more you are likely to have enough context to decipher what you are hearing.

Touching the Ethereal

Feeling the presence of spirits or energies is the most prevalent and often the most awakened of the psychic senses. When I have taught classes on psychic development, only some people report ease in seeing or hearing with their inner senses, but almost all report having experienced sensations on their hands, skin, or in their bodies. The real work is in developing refinement and control.

If you have attended an energy-sensing or psychic-development class, there is a very good chance that you experienced the energy ball exercise. The essence of this exercise involves vigorously rubbing the palms together, followed by pressing the hands together firmly, and then slowly separating the hands. Depending on the purpose of the class, the next instructions tend to be about either feeling or seeing the ball of energy that forms between the hands. Sometimes the ball of energy is made larger by spreading the hands. Often the exercise ends with pressing the hands together again to reabsorb the energy. Immediately after the energy ball exercise, the hands are more sensitive to feeling energy, and as such, this exercise is used as a warm-up to feeling the boundaries of another person's aura or other similar tasks. This is a reliable exercise and a good starting point, but with minor modifications, it can do much more.

The first thing to keep in mind is that your subtle bodies, or energy bodies, can be extremely flexible, malleable, and ductile. By the power of will and imagination, you can extend and reshape your aura for specific needs and purposes. Most of what we call touch involves a direct interaction between your body and the external world. Touch encompasses many things such as texture, pressure, temperature, pain, pleasure, and reactive sensations such as shivering, tickling, and tingling. The sense of touch is not uniform across your body. Some areas are highly sensitive with great resolution, whereas other areas have a sparse network of sensors.

Taking a page from Nature's book, touch is about the interaction of shapes with shapes, form with form. A cat has whiskers that amplify sensations and extend the reach of its touch. The loops and whorls of your fingerprints add just enough traction and just enough vibration as they catch across a surface that they reveal the intricacies of textures. The fine hairs on your arm catch the breeze and also rise up as goose bumps to create sensation as a signal. You have the ability to extend your aura, concentrate the receptors for fine discrimination, and give it a shape that can interact with the target of your attention.

For example, you can stretch out tendrils from your hands to feel the energy. It is easier to start at first by simply stretching the energy outward from your fingers, but you are not limited by your physical anatomy. You can create as many extensions of your aura of various shapes and sizes as your will, imagination, and endurance can provide. You can also adjust the texture of your auric extensions until they have the right friction and reactivity to match the qualities of the energy you are trying to touch. Cycling through different textures and surface qualities to match the energetic patterns that you are trying to sense will also give you a collection of data points to map out the small and the large structures in your target. Learning how to give your aura grit or smoothness as needed also has a secondary benefit of giving you additional tools for moving and shaping energy.

Subtle Smell and Taste

Odors and flavors have the power to arouse emotions, memories, and sensations that go deep down into your primal nature. The experience of smelling flowers in the presence of beneficent entities or the taste of copper and sulfur in the presence of something less pleasant is unforgettable. I once had a visit from the spirit of someone I knew when he was alive; his visit was heralded by the smell of his favorite cigar. Shortly thereafter, I saw a faint impression of his face, but the smell let me know who was approaching and also acted as a verification of his identity.

One of the virtues of psychic impressions that are experienced as taste or smell is that they are harder to fool and less prone to falsehood. Many people are not inspired to exert themselves to develop these psychic senses, since it appears as if the information gained would be of lesser utility. While it is true that sight, sound, and feeling may be more useful for dialogue and some other tasks, having a quick check on the veracity and true nature of a being or an energy is highly valuable. Psychic smell or taste can act as that quick test. It is harder to train yourself to be more open to experiencing psychic impressions as odors and flavors because your responses to them originate far below the level of waking consciousness, but it can be done. Instinct is hard to invoke. Exercises to awaken the psychic senses of smell and taste are mostly exercises in imagination. To awaken and train these senses, you must wait for opportunities.

The next time you are having a vivid experience with your psychic senses, usually seeing or hearing, pause and focus in on what you are smelling and/or tasting. Try to tune out any smells or tastes that have a physical origin, and tune in those of a subtle nature. While it may be difficult to stimulate the psychic senses of smell and taste from a cold start, it is relatively easy to shift an active engagement of the other psychic senses to these modalities in the heat of an experience. Even if you do not succeed at first, each time you make the attempt, you are forging links in your energy and neurology that will eventually result in a fuller activation of smell and taste.

Discerning Elemental Energies

Knowledge of the Four Elements model is common because it is prevalent in the many systems of magick and ritual. If you are not familiar with the Four Elements, plenty of readily available information from print and digital sources can provide you with a basic understanding of the meaning of the Elements. The methods and exercises related to the Four Elements that you are most likely to encounter focus on their use in creating sacred space, using their power in spell work, or as a correlate in tables of correspondence, and so on.

Elemental powers are within us and surround us at all times. The Elements can also be experienced on a continuum that runs the full range from nonsentient energy to fully individuated beings. Do not confuse Elemental energy with life force, prana, chi, or whatever name you use to describe the enlivening and ensouling energy of beings who, whether or not they have physical bodies, come from one of the life-streams of evolution. Because the Four Elements are ubiquitous, your ability to discern their qualities and actions has a significant impact on your efforts at psychic perception. Depending on the circumstances and the information being sought, sometimes you need to tune out the Elemental energy because it is the noise, not the signal. At other times, you need to tune in the Elemental energy when it contains or is the carrier for what is sought. Additionally, distinguishing the Four Elements as separate patterns is also important for clarifying perceptions.

A simple and straightforward exercise can help refine your perception of Elemental energy patterns. First, collect together four objects that will represent the Elements and act as anchors for their energy.

- For the Element of Air, you may wish to use a feather or a folding fan.
- For the Element of Fire, a lit candle or a small oil or alcohol lamp will do.
- For the Element of Water, use a clear glass bowl, tumbler, or wineglass filled with water.
- For the Element of Earth, pick an interesting-looking stone or a crystal.

Feel free to make substitutions for these objects based on your intuition and preferences. Do not use salt to represent Earth because salt has a very specific energy. For Fire, be sure to use an actual flame because an electric candle or some other simulated fire will not work well.

Place the objects in front of you on a table or counter. Look at them carefully with the intention of remembering them clearly so you can envision them when you shut your eyes later in the exercise. Then pick up the Air object and move it gently so you can feel how it moves air and interacts with air. Fan yourself so you can feel the small breeze it creates. Move on to the Fire object and bring your fingers close to the flame so you can feel the heat. Gaze upon the flame and, in particular, look at the dimmest part that is the portal near the wick. Shift your attention to the Water object and gently rock it so that the water swirls in the container. Watch the water move as it settles back to stillness. Lastly, pick up the Earth object and feel its heft and its texture in your hand. Place the stone down with enough force so that you hear a thud or click; pause and be aware of your memory of the sound and the silence that follows.

Now repeat the sequence with a goal of calling and awakening their corresponding Elemental forces. Begin by thinking about the characteristics that you attribute to Air. Take a deep breath, pulling in energy with that breath, and blow power into the Air object. Then think about the characteristics that you attribute to Fire. Rub your hands together and feel the friction heat build between them. Hold your hands near the flame and send your heat into the flame. Take your hands away from the flame and pause for a moment. Now think about the characteristics that you attribute to Water. Place your fingertips where you can feel your heartbeat; the pulse points at the wrists, throat, or temples are easiest to find for most people. Feel your pulse and imagine the circulation of blood in your body. Dip a finger into the water and feel your pulse move through the water. Dry your finger; then think about the characteristics that you attribute to Earth. Pick up the stone and hold it tightly, pushing your sense of the Element of Earth into it. Place the stone back down and pause for a moment.

Close your eyes and look toward the place where the Air object is located. Envision it as sharply as you can; then let your visualization fade slowly until what remains to be seen is the Elemental energy anchored there. Make note of the similarities and the differences between the physical appearance and the subtle appearance of the object. The energy pattern is generally larger than the physical object, so search around the anchor object as well. Repeat this process for the remaining three anchor objects while making an effort to observe how each of the Elemental energy patterns is unique and distinctive. Immediately after the exercise, take time to jot down your observations. If you are so inclined after a short rest, you may run through the energy observations again. You may omit the preparatory steps if the objects still have an Elemental charge.

After a day, or at the least a few hours, you may repeat this exercise, but this time with a focus on a different sensory modality. Instead of trying to see the Elemental energy, try to hear the energy pattern. You can do the same with smell and taste, but the process needs a slight modification for attempts to feel the energy. To avoid knocking things over and risking injury, open your eyes and position your hands near the objects, after which you can close your eyes and make an effort to feel the energy.

The next step is to observe more than one Elemental pattern simultaneously. You may have already done this inadvertently in your earlier efforts, since the anchor objects are near to each other and your field of perception may have caught them in your peripheral perception. You may wish to stand and move your angle of perception or move the objects so that their patterns overlap. Spend some time observing how the different Elemental patterns interact with each other.

When you are ready to move on to something more challenging, you can experiment with opening several sensory modalities at once. What I mean by this is extending your inner senses to see and hear the Elemental patterns, or any combination of the physical senses, as a means of making sense of your psychic perceptions.

CHAPTER 2

The Engine of Memory: Opening the Far Memory

Introduction

We can easily underestimate how much of our waking consciousness, our awareness, is built atop a foundation made of memories. For example, when we walk into a friend's living room, we recognize that the sofa is a sofa and, if we have sat on it before, how it will feel. If the friend is in the room, we recognize their face and we know why we've come that day and that moment.

Our stream of consciousness is guided by the unbidden and unnoticed memories and knowledge that inform our sense of what is occurring in the moment, our ability to identify what is going on. Without the context provided by preconscious memories, we would be like infants with the capacity for sight, but with no comprehension. By far, the largest portion of what we know and what we find intelligible is in our memories; only the tiniest fraction of our knowledge is present in our conscious awareness in any given moment. In fact, only so much *fits* within normal waking consciousness, so it is a necessity that the context-giving memories be held adjacent to, but not in our awareness. It is a marvel how quickly and seamlessly the information that we need is brought forth, swapped out with the next piece that is needed, or brought directly before our mind's eye when requested.

How is this marvel accomplished? We have the impression that our waking consciousness is a smooth and continuous stream of thoughts and percepts, but this is more a functional illusion than truth. When a movie is displayed at sixteen frames per second or faster, most people see continuous motion rather than separate still images. In the old days of actual film, there was a line between each image as well as sprocket holes along the edges that were used to align and move the film. Good evidence from scientific research suggests that our sense of waking consciousness has a frame rate. Between each frame of awareness, intensive unconscious processing occurs, a dark line we do not see. More accurately, it is more like an entire frame rather than a line that goes unseen. During that frame that is unconscious processing, our sensory information, memory, knowledge, and more are resolved into the frames of consciousness that we experience. This unconscious processing compiles, filters, and prioritizes this enormous volume of material into the most succinct and salient form that can fit within the frame of our awareness.

The unconscious period between frames of awareness is also where and when we process psychic or spiritual impressions. When we have an experience that we categorize as psychic or spiritual, it means that the experience has made it past the unconscious filters and into our awareness. Psychic development is not so much the development of the subtle senses—they are already there—but it is the development of conscious awareness of those senses. Some of the techniques to open the psychic senses are actually aimed at changing the template, the filters, the sorting algorithm, used by the unconscious self. Others aim to move information from the preconscious state into full awareness. This task has many other approaches, but I'd like to share one that uses the power of memory to enhance psychic awareness.

There are many kinds and categories of memory, but it has been my experience that the mechanism for the retrieval of memory is the same. I think this applies to the preconscious memories we use in making sense of the world, the volitional recall of facts, and the recollection of life history. I like to call this mechanism *the engine of memory* because it reminds me of an internal and invisible version of the search engines we use for the Internet. Whether or not the concept of the engine of memory holds up to scientific scrutiny is not relevant to our purposes—though I believe that it may—it does give us an idea that we can invoke. We can ask the engine of memory to include the memories of psychic and subtle perceptions in both our preconscious and conscious efforts to perceive the subtle world.

I would also like to posit that the engine of memory, when it is set to search through memories of psychic impressions, is not limited to the linear flow of time. Moreover, it can take you to times, places, and planes of reality of which you have no conscious recollection. Although distant from your *normal* consciousness, the part of you that is eternal spirit remembers the places and planes you lived in before you were born and to where you will return. Your eternal self remembers all the people and beings that you have known in this life and beyond. Your eternal self can read the journey of millennia encoded in your blood and bones. In many ways, the Universe is also a great mind, and to the degree that you can create a clear connection, you can access those memories as well. The engine of memory is what gives us access to what is called the *far memory*, the memory of things that are remembered by other minds from other times and places.

Using the Engine of Memory

To make use of the engine of memory, you must first become aware of how it feels to remember things. Since much of the function of the engine of memory is outside waking consciousness, attempting to access and influence it through visualization is not effective as a first step. The goal is to develop a kinesthetic and proprioceptive awareness of the engine of memory first. In our physical bodies, our sense of kinesthesia relates primarily to the motion of our body parts and proprioception to our sense of the relative positions of our body parts. If you close your eyes and can touch your nose with your finger, you have just used your senses of kinesthesia and proprioception with your body cooperating with your will. With some practice and patience, you'll be able to use your engine of memory just as readily.

Begin by taking ten to thirty index cards or pieces of paper and writing a prompt on each one for a specific memory that you have. These memories can be things like the face of one of your friends in high school, your first bicycle, a favorite park, a scene from a movie that you enjoy, and so on. Write one memory prompt on each card. Try to cover as broad a range of years as you can in selecting the memories. Then shuffle the cards together and either place them facedown on a table or hold them so that the writing faces away from you.

Next, you will read one of the cards, but before doing so, become aware of your physical sensations. Close your eyes, breathe, and take stock of your state of being. Then flip one of the cards and read it. Try to feel the process of the memory being brought into awareness. Pay close attention because this is something that we ignore as completely as the blinking of our eyes. In addition to your kinesthetic and proprioceptive impressions, concentrate on the way in which the memory appears in your mind. Which sensory impressions are sharpest in the recollection? Which sensory impressions are more muted in the recollection? Repeat the process with four to five more cards and then stop and contemplate the similarities between each of the efforts. Then wait a day before repeating the process. After you have completed this exercise for a week, it is time to take the next step.

Once again, shuffle the cards and proceed as you did before, but when you flip a card to read it, try to slow down the speed at which the memory takes form in your conscious awareness. Continue in your efforts to get a feel for how and where the engine of memory moves within you. When you experience a process as slowed down, it actually means that you have sped up your awareness. In this heightened state, search for more details and sensations related to your engine of memory. Follow this course of practice for a week. If you have a friend that can shuffle and read the cards to you, it would be a useful change of pace as they can report on their perceptions of your energy as well. At the end of the week, if you think you have succeeded in this part of the exercise, move on to the next step. If not, then stay the course for another week. In either case, it is time to make a fresh set of memory prompt cards.

Now that you have a better sense of your engine of memory, when you receive a prompt, try to imagine that you are feeling the movement of your engine of memory as if it were your muscles, bones, and sinew. Depending on your temperament, you may wish to move your hands, change your posture, or move your body in some other way to stimulate a linkage between the control you have over your body and your control of the engine of memory. Work to strengthen and refine your feel, your sense, of the engine of memory so that you identify it to be a part of yourself as fully as you would your hands. If you are less kinesthetic, or body aware, then it may be useful at this point to associate a sound or shape to your engine of memory. After doing this several times over the course of several days, you may be ready to apply the engine of memory in divination and psychic endeavors.

The method is the same whether you are using divinatory tools such as tarot cards, reading an astrological chart or a skrying mirror, or using pure psychism without physical instruments. First, stimulate your awareness of the engine of memory, move or shift your physical body if it helps, imagine the sound and shape of the engine, and then try to *remember* the answer to the question before you. You may receive the answer a piece at a time like reading one card at a time, or you may receive the whole answer at once. If you are looking into a skrying mirror or using pure psychism, let the recollection build up layer by layer, and let each detail reveal a more comprehensive answer. If you have the belief that the information has been retrieved but is not registering in your conscious awareness, try again but slow down the process. The information may have flickered too quickly in and out of your mind's grasp. It may be useful to use the trick of prompting yourself with a known memory and slowing how it unfolds in your mind as a way of instructing the engine of memory to deliver the requested divinatory information at a better pace. Then try to seek the information that you need again.

The basic principles of using the engine of memory are fairly straightforward, but this technique requires practice and persistence to achieve good results. As you continue to work with the engine of memory, you will find that the range and clarity of the information that is retrieved become greater. You can also begin to guide the search with more parameters. For example, you can direct the search to follow the river of blood of your ancestry. When you are reading a book or a ritual outline and are unclear on the meaning or rationale, at your behest, your bidding command, you can search for the meaning. The limitations on what you can explore are just the limits of your creativity. As is true with any method of psychism or mind magick, what you glean may be incomplete, distorted by your suppositions, or the situation may be still in flux. Regardless of these limitations, it is a useful technique to extend your capabilities.

The Silver Arrow

Because you are a microcosm, a small reflection, of the macrocosm that is the Universe and all its planes of existence, the engine of memory is also like a map and a compass. If you engage in shamanic journeying, soul flight, sending, astral projection, or other forms of spirit travel, then you can also adapt the engine of memory to assist you in those travels.

Once you have established a strong knowing for how the engine feels and where it moves within your awareness, you can begin the process of making a representational connection between it and a chosen symbol. The symbolic object I use for this purpose is a silver arrow, not a sketchy glyph of an arrow, but one that has weight, that has texture in my hand as I imagine holding it, and glints as light plays over the point, shaft, and feathers.

In my mind, the feel for the engine of memory is overlapped with a silver arrow that I grip with all my senses. I concentrate on the locus, the name, or intention of what I am seeking, and I allow the silver arrow to pull me there. My center of awareness clings to the silver arrow as it flies up, down, through, under, over, or however is needed to be at the place in time, space, and level of reality that is the arrow's target.

I also use the silver arrow to transport me to places in the other realms that I know well, if I need to be there quickly. As an example, this is one of my preferred ways to go to astral temples. Furthermore, I find that when I travel using the arrow, I seem to be more fully, more tangibly, present at my destinations. You can also use the silver arrow in conjunction with other practices. If you are in a ritual, or scanning a room or landscape, and your psychic senses seem unclear, use the silver arrow to rise on the planes until your psychic senses become clear. I have also used this technique to augment meditative and contemplative practices. Memory-enhancing systems such as the memory palace or the method of loci can be used with the silver arrow as an adjunct to these practices, since they both arise from motion and spatial memory.

Should you not like the image of a silver arrow, you can substitute any other object that is mobile and makes symbolic sense to you. For example, some people may prefer the image of a witch's broom, a flying carpet, or winged sandals.

I would caution against using the image of a living thing, such as a winged horse, because when you view something as a living thing, there is the possibility of inadvertently giving it unplanned qualities, such as a sense of autonomy. The engine of memory or variations on it like the silver arrow can become less reliable if they become too much like variations on artificial elementals or servitors. If you are not familiar with the concepts of artificial elementals or servitors, you can find many books, articles, and blogs on these topics to fill in gaps in your knowledge. This work is not about budding off a portion of your will or investing energy in an externalized construct; it is about gaining access to something that is inherently yours.

CHAPTER 3

The Three Selves

Numerous systems describe the human psyche as consisting of a set of functional components that make up the whole. This description is comparable to the sorts of classifications that you see in the study of biology or anatomy. I am making that comparison because, ultimately, it is one whole of which the division into parts is simply a means of understanding the function of the whole.

No agreement exists between the various systems on exactly how many parts, divisions, and layers there may be, nor should there be. Each method of division is valid for the purposes and the goals of the system that it serves. In music and in art, there are many perfectly workable schemes for dividing up sound and light into keys and color wheels. Some variation on the threefold Self, a tripartite division of the psyche into something akin to the primary colors, shows up in a wide range of traditions. Knowledge of the Three Selves is very useful for gaining access to and control of the inner senses.

Lest you be confused, I'd like to start by pointing out that higher is not better. Often an implicit prejudice associates up as good and down as bad. All three of the Selves are of equal importance in and of themselves. Healthy spiritual evolution requires working with and honoring all the parts that make up your psyche. You can imagine the Three Selves as being three pistons, three cylinders, and the engine of your being. When the Three Selves are in sync with each other, you progress down the path smoothly. When they are not, the journey is experienced as rough even if the way is smoothly paved.

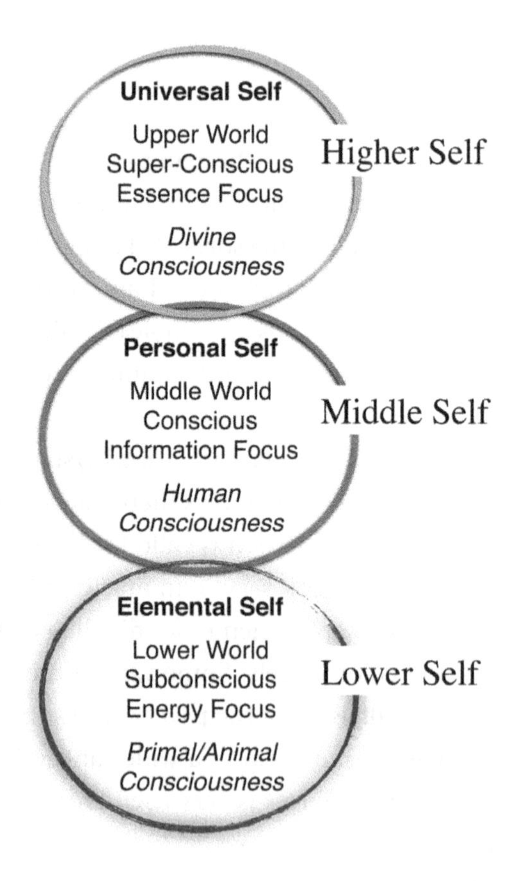

I refer to the Three Selves numerous times in this book. Some exercises and practices are geared to developing your awareness of the Three Selves as well. Awareness can lead to integration and/or better collaboration between these three styles of consciousness. You will find mention or discussion of the Three Selves model under a variety of names in shamanism, Victor and Cora Anderson's line of Witchcraft, psychology, the Western Mystery Traditions, Hawaiian Huna, several New Age philosophies, and Qabala, among other disciplines. My initial encounter with this model was in my studies of Qabala, the Tree of Life, where the Three Selves, respectively, are the *Nephesh*, *Ruach*, and *Neshamah*, which are a subset of a more elaborate model.

At first, you may find that some of the descriptions of the Three Selves and their symbols may clash when comparing different systems. With a bit of contemplation and consideration of the aims and purposes of different systems, you can usually find a way to harmonize how the Three Selves appear when viewed from their vantage points.

The Lower Self

The bulk of your psychic gifts and intuition reside in and arise from your Lower Self. This portion of the Self experiences reality in as close to a continuous flow as is possible for a human being. This is the predominant Self when you are dreaming and visioning. This is the part of you wherein the unconscious, the subconscious, and the preconscious dance with each other and create much of what you perceive of both the physical world and the subtle realms. This is also the part of you that manages the collection and distribution of the energies that come in from the world and shape them into the life force that is woven into your physical body and your aura. The Lower Self is the elemental Self and is the seat of primal consciousness. It is strongly connected to your animal consciousness, your genetics, and your bloodline.

The Lower Self is the part of you that is most present in the Underworld. The Lower Self is more strongly connected to the lower chakras and the layers of the aura closest to the physical body. As such, it does the heavy lifting in most psychic or magickal work.

The Lower Self's mode of consciousness, and its way of experiencing reality, is holographic in nature. A hologram is a whole picture in the sense that it captures all three dimensions, unlike the two dimensions of photography. High-quality holograms, not the small, cheap ones on credit cards and such, can be viewed from multiple angles to even see objects that are obscured by other objects. The plate that the hologram is captured on is filled with complex interference and diffraction patterns of light waves bouncing off the objects and interacting with each other. In a similar fashion to how a well-done audio recording captures the musicians, their relative locations, and also the ambience of the hall, a hologram captures the whole space. Usually, a hologram has to be illuminated in a particular way for the patterns to be reconstructed and become visible. Every part of a hologram is informed by what is going on in the rest of the hologram because it is made of the combination of all the wave fronts.

The Lower Self knows the truth of the statement that all things are connected and that separation is an illusion, because its mode of experiencing reality is of sensing its place in the overlapping wave fronts in the field of being. The Lower Self knows things that are obscured or beyond the range of its senses, but it feels them through the web of interactions. When the light of the Middle Self illuminates the perceptions of the Lower Self in the right way, the information becomes visible and intelligible in our normal waking consciousness.

The Middle Self

Your Middle Self is reading this page. This is the seat of normal waking consciousness, language, and reasoning. This is the voice of your thoughts, memories, and much of what you consider your personal identity; it is the personal Self. The Middle Self focuses on information; it divides the stream of reality into words, symbols, and discrete objects. The Middle Self looks for the connections, relationships, and patterns that form the whole.

Often, the Middle Self is viewed as an obstacle to psychic or spiritual pursuits because it is the part of the psyche that most clearly perceives the physical world. However, the Middle Self is also the center of the higher mind that produces eureka moments and leaps of understanding when it is properly developed. The center, the middle of things, is the place where the above and the below can meet and be integrated.

The Middle Self is more strongly connected to the middle chakras and the central layers of the aura. The Middle Self is the part of you that is most present in the Middle World. Take note that though associated with the powers of the mind, the Middle Self is strongly connected to the Heart Chakra. Knowing is required for what is identified as human consciousness and also for personal love.

The Middle Self's mode of consciousness is based primarily on the Microcosm–Mesocosm–Macrocosm pattern—the small-, the middle-, and the large-scale order of things best expressed as the Hermetic Axiom of "as above, so below, but in a different manner." The world is seen as wheels within wheels, as systems within systems, with rules and guidelines extending into all the domains that can be perceived. This is the perspective that allows us to make sense of the world and to extrapolate outcomes. Much of what we call metaphysics—the sacred sciences such as astrology, laws of magick, tables of correspondences, and the like—are products of the Middle Self's style of consciousness. The Middle Self presides over the part of spiritual, psychic, and magickal practices that involve steps, procedures, ritual, and symbolic representation.

The Higher Self

The Higher Self is tethered in time to your incarnation, to your passage through this life, and yet resides in eternity. The Higher Self is your Divine spark, your drop from the Sea of Universal Being, and is the part of you that remains when your physical life is done. The Higher Self is the universal Self and is the seat of Divine consciousness within you. It is focused on the essence of things, and its knowing and understanding arise from the power of like calling to like. The Divine spark of the Higher Self recognizes that Divine spark in all other things. The mode of consciousness of this part of Self is difficult to translate into the word-based consciousness of the Middle Self because it is highly concentrated and multilayered. It is often easier for information to be passed from the Higher Self to the Lower Self as images, both still and moving, that can convey more than words. Then material from the Lower Self arises into the reach of the Middle Self. This is a common workaround process, but the goal is integration and direct communion between the Three Selves. The Higher Self is more strongly connected to the upper chakras, the outer layers of the aura, and our connection to universal consciousness. The Higher Self is the part of you that is most present in the Upper World.

In 1975, the mathematician and polymath Benoit Mandelbrot coined the term *fractal* as he explored both roughness and self-similarity of shapes in nature through the lens of mathematics and his powerful imagination. Today, numerous kinds of fractal equations are used to study and to model complexity in nature and chaos. A remarkably brief fractal equation produces the portion of the Mandelbrot set visualized here. It is only a portion, because it is the nature of fractals to have ever-growing or evolving symmetry with repeating patterns that can be exact, quasi-similar, statistically similar, and more complex possibilities. If you have seen the patterns of frost on a window or snowflakes, you have seen fractals expressed in the physical plane. The branching pattern of trees is fractal, as are the waves in the ocean. Fractal patterns are found in physical objects, in sounds, in the interaction of electromagnetic fields, and in a wide range of spatial and temporal arrangements in the natural world.

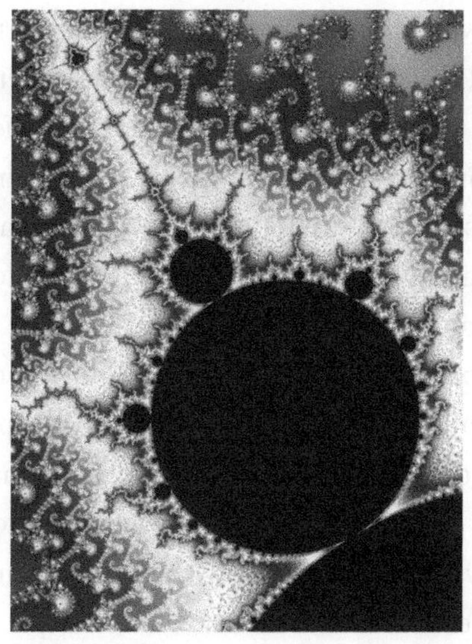

$$f_c(z) = z^2 + c$$

So, what does this have to do with the Higher Self? The Higher Self is focused on the essence of things, and fractals are a good comparison for how spirit becomes a force that becomes the ever-evolving and differentiating reality of the manifest world. In the same manner that it can be said that the Middle Self *thinks* in words, the Higher Self can be said to *think* in fractals. The Higher Self knows what shapes the patterns that you experience.

The Shadows of the Three Selves

Remember when I said that upper doesn't mean better than lower? The term *shadow* is frequently laden with negative connotations because of the duality of dark and light often being used as code for evil and good. The dark of the womb and rich soil nurture life. The dark of night gives us rest and a time for love. The blistering sun of noon in the summer is not kindly.

Use of the word *shadow* as a psychological term and concept was developed by Carl Gustav Jung and has been adopted into many spiritual systems as well. The shadow is more than unresolved fears, hidden memories, traumas, or other suppressed things; it is also those things that are intrinsically obscure or beyond our capacity to understand. The shadow is also the home of all that is ineffable, the mysteries. Fear of the shadow is probably more dangerous and causes more personal distortion than accepting its full reality. Much of your personal power and beauty is rooted in and nourished by your shadow. Imagine how restricted artists would be if they were limited to only light and no shadows. Imagine music without the silences that create rhythm and the duration of notes.

When you contemplate the Three Selves, or any other model describing the psyche, remember that each part of the

Self has its own version of the shadow. More often than not, much of what is thought of as the shadow is conflated with the Lower Self; primal consciousness contains but does not solely consist of the shadow. The shadow of toxic thought patterns is cast by the Middle Self. The shadow of blurred boundaries is cast by the Higher Self. All the parts of Self have lights, shadows, and more that we are yet to know or name. Just as one of the goals in spiritual development is the integration of the Three Selves, so is the integration of the shadow of each part. In fact, I believe that the shadow is the matrix of the Self, the connective tissue that joins the parts, the night sky within that lets our stars shine. If it is a part of your being, then it is a part of the Universe within you.

Clairs and Noirs

I was recently asked how it was possible for someone who had limited or no apparent psychic ability to lead a ritual or a working. I should also add the context of the ritual in question was one that involved operative magick rather than devotional work. In other words, how could a person who was seemingly head-blind be capable of weaving together the energies that were being directed toward them in the ritual?

How does a person who does not perceive subtle forms and subtle energies know whether or not the circle, or whatever magical container she's created, is actually solid and secure? How does this person know if any existing imbalances need to be corrected? And lastly, how does this person know if the work has truly been done? I will be honest and say that if someone had posed that question to me a few decades ago, I would have said that it was not possible. And I would have been wrong in making that summary judgment.

It was an abundance of psychic experiences that drew me to magick and Paganism at an early age. Learning to distinguish what was real physically from what was real in the subtle realms and what was pure imagination was an essential part of my development as a person. So in my early days, I could not imagine a person who did not perceive as I did being a competent practitioner. Of course, I knew that different individuals would convert their psychic impressions into different symbols or different sensory modalities. Some people are stronger at seeing, others at hearing, others feeling, and so on, but I still had the assumption that they were using their psychic perceptions to guide their spiritual and magickal efforts.

My first inkling that the conscious perception of energy was not always necessary for effective workings actually came in a non-magickal setting. Years ago, while in college, I was making the rounds with my artsy and avant-garde friends in a night filled with lots of performance poetry, cheap wine and cheese, kinetic art, and lastly an unconventional dance troupe. Much of what I saw was interesting and inventive but didn't really catch my attention. Then a dancer came on stage by herself, and to my eyes, she was surrounded with a nimbus and shifting lights. My first thought was that she was a priestess, as I'd seen that type of aura before. When she danced, I saw her juggle flames and bring down a rain of stars that turned and spread to a series of crashing waves whose foam spread across the stage. At the after party, I asked her about her performance and started to describe what I had seen. Her eyes grew large, and she told me that the imagery I described was very close to what she had envisioned in creating the piece that she danced. She also grew really uncomfortable because she was not a magickal person and had no awareness that she was projecting or creating those forms so palpably.

The proof of the pudding is in the eating. I have observed powerful rituals and workings with tangible effects from practitioners that by their own accounts don't sense much of anything when they work. I have been the recipient of effective healings from healers who cannot describe nor explain how they know what to do when they offer healing touch or prayers. In training students, I can think of several who can create powerful sacred space, but claim to feel and see nothing. I have also had students that see and sense so well that they think they have cast a proper circle, when there is only a wispy tracery of energy. I find it notable that often my good students, of the sort who seem not to have psychism, more often report a sense of when things have a "rightness" to them, whereas my students who rely on their psychic senses tend not to report a deep knowing as a measure of their work.

In the current spiritual and magickal culture, there is a great emphasis on seeing and on all of the *clairs*, as I like to call them. Most of you are familiar with words like *clairvoyance*, *clairaudience*, *clairsentience*, and other words that are used to label the psychic senses. *Clair* is a French word that means light or clear or distinct. So the commonly described psychic senses are really just those that we experience in our waking consciousness. This is an important distinction that I believe begins to explain how it is possible to do spiritual work without conscious perception of subtle energies.

In my work, I have also coined the concept of psychic senses that are *noirs*, after the French word for black or dark. As an example, automatic writing or the use of a pendulum for divination requires the use of the noirs. When someone is engaged in automatic writing, they do not first hear or see the words in their consciousness; instead, they read them and discover them as they write them.

Normal waking consciousness, the part of you that is reading this book, is only a portion of your being. I would also argue that even waking consciousness is only a subset of the Middle Self. Much of our awareness of subtle energies, spirits, and other planes of being arises from or is resident in our Lower Self and our Higher Self.

Those people who experience psychic perception in their waking consciousness are translating those impressions that are received in other parts of the Self into the symbols that can be understood by what we have named as conscious awareness. When people are performing divination, healings, and the like without conscious awareness, they are allowing other parts of their being to take charge of their efforts. This is not unconscious action or decision making; rather, it is the turning over of control to other parts of our being that also have the capacity for judgment. Much of this unseen wisdom comes from the shadow of the Three Selves.

I do believe that all human beings have psychic senses and that these senses vary in acuity, just as the physical senses do. The greatest amount of difference lies in how much integration there is between the different parts of the Self and how focus and the executive function are shared between different kinds of consciousness. I still believe that most people can develop the ability to perceive the subtle realms in their waking consciousness. However, as I pointed out earlier, that is no guarantee that their work will be any better than that performed by those who are allowing instinct and their noirs to guide their actions. However, those who do not have conscious psychic perception generally do better if they are trained by people who have psychism.

Even though I do have very sharp psychic senses, I have found that some of my most powerful work has occurred when my hand has moved on its own, when my voice has shifted to a sound that I did not choose, and so on. For those who do have the clairs, it is important to learn how to relinquish control to the noirs. For those who desperately want to see, it may or may not come to pass, but it is not the measure of your worth as a practitioner. I said earlier that the proof of the pudding is in the eating, and it behooves you not to skip any of the layers.

CHAPTER 4

Divination, Prophecy, and Oracular Vision

A significant amount of psychic work is directed toward seeking information and guidance. A great number of words and terms are used to describe this practice, and often many of these words are used interchangeably, as approximate synonyms for each other by practitioners. I have found it useful to create fairly sharp distinctions between a number of these words to designate different approaches that involve different modes and subsequently different outcomes. If you consult dictionaries and encyclopedias, you will not find an exact match to the definitions that I offer. After reading this chapter, you may or may not choose to adopt my terminology, but I hope that you will understand the value in making these distinctions. From my perspective, divination, prophecy, and oracular vision are three related but discrete methodologies for acquiring information from unseen and subtle sources. What all three have in common is that there is a focus on information that is some distance away from the present moment in either the past or the future.

Divination

Divination can be compared to a weather forecast, in that it predicts the most probable outcome based on what can be sensed at the time of the question. Weather forecasts are most accurate in the near term and diminish in accuracy in the long term. Divination is the determination of the most probable timeline. Sometimes the line to the most probable future is a deeply ingrained groove with other possible futures, barely visible scratches on the surface of probability. At other junctures, the most probable future is only slightly more likely than two or three other contending timelines. The act of divination can and often does change the probabilities, as the information gained through divination changes both perspectives and choices from that moment onward. If that were not the case, very few people would be interested in divination at all.

At any given moment, a person has a certain amount of awareness of their world, a quantity of power, and some level of will and determination to apply their choices. The individual's actions and inputs to shape the flow of the future are combined with, summed with, those from other living beings, spirits, and natural forces to produce the future that becomes actual rather than potential. The scale of a question also has an impact on the information obtained through divination in addition to the span of time involved. The larger the scale and span of the question, the more contributors to the shaping of the outcome that figuratively gives more inertia and momentum to the most probable timeline. It is fairly rare for the most probable outcome to be the best and most optimal future. When you are fortunate, divination provides information early enough so you can begin to brake and to steer in a different direction. This is easier to do on a bicycle than on a cargo ship. Sometimes divination serves as a warning to be prepared to cope because the two or three most probable futures all contain unwanted outcomes.

Prophecy

More often than not, prophecy is associated with religions, as it is seen as guidance from God/dess/es or beings sent by them. The person receiving the message is in effect a spokesperson for a spiritual entity that appeared to them, communicated with them, and/or caused the inspiration for the message to appear in their psyche. The phrase "self-fulfilling prophecy," coined by sociologist Robert K. Merton, illuminated how the power of expectation and belief can affect behaviors enough to bring a prophecy into manifestation. For my purposes, I define all prophecy as self-fulfilling, but in addition to sociological and psychological forces, spiritual forces also are involved. Unlike divination, which shows the most probable futures, prophecy seeks the less likely but more beneficial futures. Moreover, prophecy suggests ways to navigate from the wide road that is the main timeline to the back roads, the lesser timelines, to avoid obstacles and arrive at a different destination.

At first glance, prophecy sounds more useful than divination, but each mode has its strengths and drawbacks. Prophecy always has an agenda, an axe to grind, and the selection of a better future is defined by the ethos, tenets, and personality of the source of the guidance. What is good from one perspective may be seen to create other problems from another perspective. In addition, there are always unintended consequences. What constitutes a better future is always focused on specific individuals or communities within the context of their values. If there was assistance from a spiritual entity in the selection of the path forward to this better future, the spirit's perspectives and purposes are also taken into consideration. Prophecy, as I'm defining it, still contains a self-fulfilling aspect in that those who have received the guidance will endeavor to follow it. Prophecy is also a psychic or a supernatural act in that it finds the turning points in the future that are needed to veer onto the timeline that leads to the desired rather than the most probable outcomes.

Oracular Vision

The Oracle of Delphi, the Pythia, is perhaps the best known of the ancient oracles, although by my definitions, her utterances would most frequently be classified as divination or prophecy. Often the words of oracles are viewed as ambiguous, obscure, and difficult to interpret. Indeed, in the case of the Pythia, priests helped in the interpretation of the Oracle's words.

In some instances, the Oracle's words were neither divination nor prophecy, but rather would fall into the category that I define as oracular vision. In the practices of both divination and prophecy, much of the psychic perception is focused on the ever branching and shifting strands of possibility that are the timelines that lead to possible futures. Divination maps the strongest of these lines to the future, and prophecy determines the value of each of these lines.

Oracular vision is a summarization of the entire field of action that is shaping the timelines and their relative probabilities. The information and guidance provided through oracular vision are particularly dense and difficult to unpack, not because they are ambiguous or unclear but rather because they are packed with condensed information. Oracular vision can also be likened to a collection of elegant equations that describe the metaphysics of how the future unfolds relative to the questions posed.

The value of this mode of guidance is that it gives the opportunity to understand all the underlying forces and patterns that shape outcomes, thus providing the potential to create new turning points, new junctures, for change that would otherwise not come into being. If you have the wisdom to understand the oracular vision, and the resources to act on the opportunities that are revealed, then you can add lines to the future that did not exist before your intervention. Rather than coping with the hand that you've been dealt, you have the opportunity to rummage through the deck and pick the card that you need. Although it would seem as if this is the best of the three modes described, it is also the most difficult to use. The learning curve is steep, and if you take a misstep, the fall off that curve is sharp. To use oracular vision well requires a great deal of knowledge of how the mundane world works as well as the world of spirit.

Relationship to the Three Selves

Although potentially the whole of your being is used whenever you engage in any of these three modes, affinities also exist between the Three Selves and divination, prophecy, and oracular vision. The Lower Self is most strongly connected to the practice of divination. The Middle Self is most strongly connected to the practice of prophecy. The Higher Self is most strongly connected to the practice of oracular vision.

A stacking, a sequential relationship, also exists between these modes of guidance. The Lower Self's power of instinct and sensitivity to the flow of possibilities empower divination. Of the three modes, divination requires only itself to function effectively. The Middle Self's power of discernment, communication, and planning takes what has been divined to then generate prophecy. The Higher Self's capacity to merge with and to know more expansive states of reality provides the basis for oracular vision, but this becomes productive only when the powers of divination and prophecy are also engaged. The more integrated you are as a person and as a practitioner, the more all three of the Selves will coordinate in efforts at divination, prophecy, and oracular vision.

Knowing the affinities of the Selves to divination, prophecy, and oracular vision can also help you determine the type of information and guidance that you are receiving. By examining your sensations and finding which of the Three Selves is the most active, you have a strong indicator for whether you are engaged in divination, prophecy, or oracular vision. Furthermore, if you need to shift from one mode to another, you can do so by moving your focus of consciousness and energy to the Self that corresponds to the desired mode. For most people, there is also an association with rising on the planes of being, from denser to more rarified, that is related to the movement from divination to prophecy to oracular vision. By moving your center of consciousness, your focus of being, up or down within the central column of energy aligned with your spine, you can prepare yourself to access the mode that best suits the task at hand.

Choosing and Using the Right Mode

Divination is the most common mode because it takes the least effort and preparation, while providing useful guidance for events that are in the near future. Sometimes when you are hurried and the guidance is needed quickly, in those situations divination is the best option. If you are not in the midst of a quickly evolving situation, or have decided to also begin to make longer-term plans, then the mode of prophecy becomes more useful. I've also seen readings using tools such as the tarot or the runes begin as divination and then have the follow-up questions move into the mode of prophecy. For prophecy to be effective, you have to have a clear idea of what the best or most optimal outcome should be. If you don't know what would serve you best, then you need to have the guidance of someone who knows you well enough to offer a solid perspective. Alternatively, you can use the guidance of spiritual entities that have proven themselves to be reliable and wise. If you attempt prophecy without knowing what serves you well, you will get an answer, but it will not necessarily lead to what you need or what you want.

Unless you have a strong natural gift for oracular vision, it is better to begin amassing information and guidance through divination and prophecy to set the stage for the oracular work. It takes either a lot of talent or a lot of practice to be able to move swiftly into the upper planes of being and to operate through the perspective of your Higher Self. This is one of the reasons that working to achieve a regular vision often includes a ritual component. A ritual or a protocol enables you to elevate your consciousness in graded steps rather than trying to pull yourself up by your bootstraps. It is like the difference between trying to climb a knotted rope to reach the second story of a house or taking the stairs to reach the same place. If you have access to people or groups that engage in oracular practices, you may wish to study with them or observe their practices. That said, there is nothing wrong with thinking through your own process, your own practices, and designing a ritual that is specifically tailored to your needs and temperament.

Closing Comment

To make it easier to understand the distinctions between divination, prophecy, and oracular vision, I have emphasized them as three separate modes. Indeed, you can use them singly and have good results. In real-life practice, it is more likely that you will use a mixture of them—sometimes perhaps using all three modes in varying proportions, and at other times perhaps just two of the modes. If you find that the terms that I have selected for these three modes of gaining information and guidance do not appeal to you, create your own terms. It is important that you be aware of the qualities of the three modes and that you know which ones you are using at any given time, lest you be led astray. There are many anecdotes about the information and guidance provided by the psychic senses being used well, and just as many stories that are cautionary tales about the harm caused by misunderstanding the guidance. How you use the flowchart of the most probable futures is different from how you would use the treasure map to better futures. Different errors are made when what has been provided is prophecy, but you think that it is easy to achieve because you mistake it for the smooth and broad road of the most probable future. The utterance of the oracles is greatly misunderstood when it is treated as prose rather than as multifaceted poetry or as metaphor. Be aware of the value and power of each of these modes, and you will come closer to creating the life that you both need and want.

CHAPTER 5

Managing Psychic Sensitivity

Introduction

You can have too much of a good thing, and this is certainly true with the subtle senses. An overload of especially keen subtle senses can lead to shutting them down completely or stifling them to the point that they begin to wither. Even when the methods used to throttle down psychic sensitivity work, they often tend to diminish the quality of perceptions and impressions. Some people are born with a high level of sensitivity, others develop it through their efforts to become more sensitive, and others for no clear reason cross the line into uncomfortable sensitivity. This nonproductive sensitivity may be constant, shift randomly, or fluctuate with changes in the body, psyche, or celestial cycles. One of the goals of this chapter is to offer insights into the types and causes of psychic overload and to teach methods to maintain both comfort and clarity of perception.

Types of Overload

The first step is to develop a more nuanced sense of what is being experienced as an excess of perception, as distortion. Imagine for a moment that you are a sound engineer working in a studio trying to clean up the sound recording from a live concert. By carefully adjusting different parts of the sound spectrum, you can bring out the vocals so that they are clear and distinct. By compressing the sound in the recording, you can bring up the quiet parts so you don't strain to hear them and lower the loud parts so they aren't painful and distorted. As the sound engineer, you can do this and more because you have knowledge of how people experience different frequencies, and you have the right tools and equipment to make these adjustments.

Similarly, a digital photo can be adjusted so that the shadows, mid-tones, and highlights are in the right proportions to make the image clear and distinct. Through sensible choices, the colors in a photo can be corrected so that the colors are truer to the reality that the image represents. In both of these examples, the profile, the magnitudes, the qualities of sound, and the light are modified to better match the perceptive capacities of the individual's ears and eyes. These adjustments are often needed because microphones and cameras have a different range of sensitivities than their biological equivalents. There are significant differences between what our subtle senses and what our physical senses record. The conversion and adjustment of subtle sensory data to physical sensory data are at the core of most issues of overload or distortion.

When we are confronted with an overload of psychic perception, an intractable tangle of too much, it is often easier to cut the Gordian knot that often results in a shutting down of subtle awareness. Other options exist and, in fact, a lesser known story about the Gordian knot is applicable. In Gordium, the capital city of the ancient Anatolian nation of Phrygia, a yoke was tied to a pole, by an ancient king selected by Zeus, with a knot so intricate that none could untie it. Tradition said that whoever could untie the knot would conquer Asia. Alexander the Great undid the knot. In the most popular version of the story, Alexander, after being confounded by the knot, sliced it with his sword. This is fitting for a bold general, but there is an alternate version of the story.

In this alternate version, Alexander, great of mind, pulled out the pin that held the yoke to the pole, pulled apart the yoke from the pole, and found the ends of the knot. He undid the knot without destroying the cord of woven bark. Psychic sensitivity is managed best by learning to unravel the knot.

Energy, Information, and Essence

Hopefully, you have been reading this book in the order in which the chapters are presented, rather than skipping about to whatever caught your interest. If you have not read the chapter on the Three Selves, do so before continuing. Many years ago, I came up with a model for describing the three basic elements or channels that apply to subtle perception, communication with spirits, and also give a different angle on the Three Selves model. I call these three Elements by the names *Energy*, *Information*, and *Essence*. I usually refer to this model as the *Elements of Being*. I have written and taught about this model in other contexts for other uses, but these elements also form a good foundation for analyzing psychic overload. I describe them here with an emphasis on their application in managing psychic sensitivity. To return for a moment to the sound engineering analogy, you can think of these three Elements as the bass, mid-tones, and treble.

Energy

When the overload is experienced as strong emotions, intense bodily sensations, interference with breathing or balance or control of your movements, and is often noticed by the people observing your reaction, more Energy is being processed than you can handle. Our experience of Energy is neither the pattern for a process nor is it a conceptualization of the pattern; it is our reaction and engagement with what is conveyed. Energy moves us. A beam of red light is red, and when we see it, we do so by absorbing some of it. Energy affects us by creating sensation and experience. Energy, used in this sense, is the carrier wave for manifestation. The Lower Self has the greatest sensitivity to Energy. When people identify as empaths who are overwhelmed by their sensitivity, it is their Lower Self experiencing an overload of Energy in the form of emotion and passion. The Energy channel has the most inherent capacity to carry power and is the most common source of overload. Energy is more closely associated with the *Nephesh*.

Information

All forms of language, both symbolic and literal, are Information in this context. When there is the experience of too many voices, too many images, or of a storm of quickly changing impressions, then the type of overload is Information. It can also be an orderly collection of facts or data, but if it is too fast, it can still cause an overload. Information can also be a sequence of interrelated actions, a process. Another component of Information is the description of relationships between things. The entire realm of conscious thought falls into this category, as our waking consciousness is a stream of summarizations. Information can be likened to summarizing statements like the laws of physical sciences. If *Information* can be compared to data and the laws and formulas of physical sciences, then *Essence* is the underlying nature that produces the phenomena that those laws and statements describe. Information is the way of knowing and state of being expressed by the microcosm–macrocosm paradigm and is both relational and reductive. Information is more closely associated with the Middle Self and the *Ruach*.

Essence

When the presence of spiritual forces or entities is so strong that it is a muffling burden, or so loud and bright that it begins to blur or blot you out, it is an Essence overload. As a general rule, this form of overload does not come from other incarnate human beings. Essence can be compared to the chromosomes in a fertilized egg or a seed in that it is the map and the director for the possibilities of development and unfolding. It is also like a mathematical formula that of itself is a small thing but produces a complicated three-dimensional graph when numbers are plugged into it. These comparisons to physical things are necessary but somewhat misleading because Essence is the least physical of the three Elements of Being.

Essence is the go-between, the intermediary between the un-manifest and the manifest, the implicate and the explicate. This is the domain of the mystic. Essence is the way of knowing and states of being expressed by fractals and chaos theory. Essence is more closely associated with the Higher Self and the *Neshamah*.

I know that grasping this model will take a while, and gaining understanding will take putting it into practice. Here's an analogy that you can keep in mind as you work your way toward understanding the three. Imagine a container filled with a richly fragrant liquid. The liquid corresponds with Energy. The container that gives shape to the liquid is the Information. The fragrance that floats above the container is the Essence. The liquid takes on the context and the style of the container while remaining itself. The juicy part is the Energy. The fragrance tells us more of the nature of the liquid and its history than even a sip of the liquid itself. Essence is the most nuanced of the three. Think of a container as thought and process made tangible. Is the container a bowl, a chalice, a mug, a pitcher, and so on? What is it made of, what is it for, and what thought went into the design? The container is an expression of Information.

As previously stated, Energy, Information, and Essence also have correlations to the Three Selves. Although the Lower, Middle, and Higher Selves each contain all three of the Elements of Being, the inherent proportions and sensitivities of the three vary. In the same way that the Four Elements model states that we are composed of a mixture of Fire, Earth, Air, and Water, imagine that the Three Selves are composed of a mixture of Energy, Information, and Essence. For the sake of simplicity, and perhaps clarity, here are somewhat arbitrary numbers to describe these proportions and sensitivities. Let's say that the Lower Self is 4 parts Energy, 2 parts Information, and 1 part Essence. Let's say that the Middle Self is 1½ parts Energy, 4 parts Information, and 1½ parts Essence. Let's say that the Higher Self is 1 part Energy, 2 parts Information, and 4 parts Essence. So what does this imply?

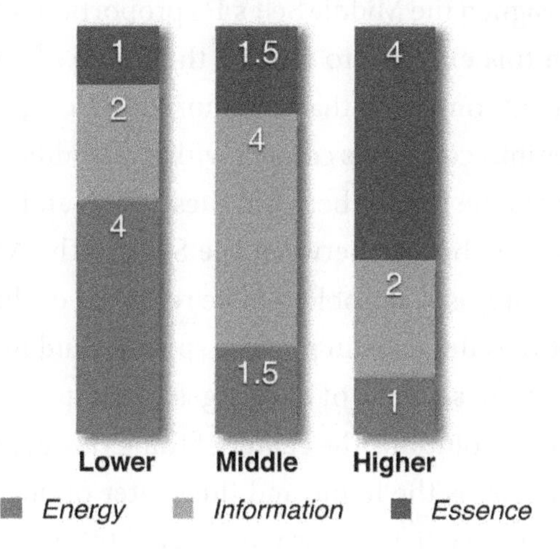

A long-standing principle in magick is that "like calls to like," and a two-way flow occurs in these linkages. In the presence of an overload of Energy, all Three Selves are affected, but the impact will be felt the strongest in the Lower Self because its largest Element is Energy. By logical extension, an overload of Information primarily affects the Middle Self, and one of Essence, the Higher Self. Because it is a two-way connection, managing an overload is best done through the Self that is most affected. The first step is to identify the type of overload. Later in this chapter, a technique delineates how this is done.

As a side note, you may wish to look at the proportions I've selected for the Three Selves. The proportions for the Lower and the Higher Selves mirror each other, and this is reflective of why it is often easier for people to get these two parts of Self to work together smoothly. Many spiritual and magickal systems and practices such as some forms of witchcraft and shamanism depend on the easy resonance between the Lower and Higher

Selves. I assigned the Middle Self's 1½ proportions of Energy and Essence in this example to suggest the rough accommodation, reduction, or conflation that is required to bring the Lower or the Higher into conscious contact with the Middle. This uneven fit represents the barrier between these types and styles of consciousness, the barrier between the Selves. The Middle Self is not broken, nor is it a problem to be removed or diminished, as it is sometimes depicted in popular spiritual and magickal writings. In fact, these types of challenges generate ego refinement and spiritual evolution. The center of things always matters, and the Middle Self is the home and the center of our incarnation. Please take notice that the proportions of Information, the primary Element of the Middle Self, in the Three Selves are either 2 or 4, suggesting that the powers of the Middle Self can bridge the heights and the depths within. Information in the form of imagination is the easiest and surest way for the Middle Self to commune and coordinate with the Lower and the Higher Self. It is not surprising that magickal and energy work techniques that are effective rely on the imagination to provide access to power and to control.

Grounding and Centering

The practice of grounding and centering is widespread in many magickal and spiritual communities. If you are unfamiliar with it, you can easily find information in books and online. I devote a chapter to grounding and centering in my book *Casting Sacred Space: The Core of All Magickal Work* (Weiser Books, 2012).

Grounding connects us to the flow of life around us so that we can take what we need and return what we do not need to the Universe. Centering helps us find and connect with the balance point within ourselves from where our consciousness interacts with the world. Often when people are having a reaction to an excess or an overload from a ritual or psychic work, they are reminded to ground and center. More often than not, this is excellent advice, as it does allow any excess that has built up to flow down out of the person and into the Earth. It also encourages the person to take a time-out to find their inner balance once more. There are many good reasons why this practice has become so popular and is one of the first steps to take in dealing with an overload.

Sometimes grounding and centering do not help and in fact may make things worse. If the person has received damage, not just an overload, then grounding and centering may just increase their exposure to the source of the problem. Let me compare this to a sunburn, as a way to convey the nature of the problem.

Almost everyone I know has at some time had a sunburn. I am ridiculously careful with sunscreen every day after having had a skin cancer scare a number of years ago. Before then, I often didn't realize that I had had too much sun until a day later, when my skin was inflamed and sensitive. I can recall times when just a fingertip running across my arm felt like someone dragging a rusty nail across my skin. There have been times when the sunburn was bad enough that even a cool, soothing balm felt like an assault on my skin. There was also, in more extreme cases, a sense of malaise. Nature often repeats certain patterns, and human nature perhaps even more often. I have often observed that what we experience in our physical bodies is similar to what we experience in our souls, our psyches, and our spirits. I think that we can get a *soulburn*, and it is very much like a sunburn.

The aura, the subtle bodies, the psyche of a person can become inflamed and sensitized by overexposure to energy, information, and essence. At that point, grounding and centering, because they maintain an open flowing connection to the flow of the environment around the person, just increase the irritation and potentially the damage.

One of the keys to healing from a sunburn is to stay out of the sunlight. The key to healing from soulburn is similar in that for a time you reduce your exposure to what is coming into your aura. It will require experimentation and self-awareness on your part to discover your symptoms and sensations, so that you'll know when you have crossed the line into soulburn. Until you can accurately determine that you are overly inflamed and sensitized, try the standard forms of grounding and centering first. If that does not help, try to remove yourself from the environment that you experience as harmful or distressing as soon as you can. I have developed an alternative form of grounding and centering that does work, even when you are past your comfort zone.

An Alternative Form of Grounding and Centering: Grounding to Yourself

In this form of grounding and centering, all the action occurs inside your own subtle bodies, your own aura. The goal of this variant is to reaffirm the normal state and balance of your energy and to recenter your identity closer to your true self. This variant of grounding and centering is useful in and of itself, as a way to step out of an overload, so that you can take stock of yourself. It also is a part of a protocol shared later in this chapter. It cannot be used as a replacement for other methods of grounding and centering because it reduces the amount of power you can draw from your environment and reduces your external psychic perceptions as well. If you used it all the time, you would become increasingly deficient in life force. This technique is more than just shielding; it helps heal and restore you after an overload.

Instructions

1. Breathe deeply and slowly. If you have any pressing concerns or worries, set them aside. Tell your troubles that you will return to them later but that for now you wish to lay your burdens down. Listen to the sounds of your surroundings, and when you are certain that all is well, tune those sounds out of your conscious awareness. Let tension seep away from your body. Let each deep, slow breath carry away all discomfort and fill you with well-being.

2. Close your eyes and move yourself inward into your core, into your inner landscape. This is your place of strength that existed before you were born. If as a part of your practice you have an inner landscape that you visit regularly, you may use that. If it is an inner temple or building, refrain from using it unless it has windows or doors that allow you to see the horizon from several directions.

3. Look around and take in the full circle of the horizon within yourself. Make note of the sights, the sounds, the smells, and anything else you may perceive. Then look at the above and the below.

4. Now see yourself becoming a tree in the center of your inner landscape. Imagine that your arms and hands are boughs and branches reaching upward toward the brilliance of your Crown Chakra. Your feet are sprouting roots that reach down toward your Root Chakra. Stay fully within the energy boundaries of yourself, your auric egg. For most people, their tree stays within their torso.

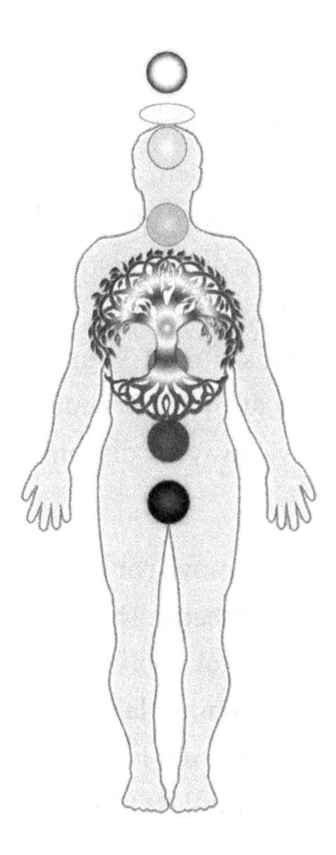

5. Feel the light of your Crown Chakra streaming down through your leaves and branches. Feel the warmth and energy of your Root Chakra rising up and feeding the roots of your tree. Pull in the power of your inner *above* and *below*. If you work with the Transpersonal Chakra, the personal Kether, then you can substitute it for the Crown Chakra.

6. Bring the light of the above and below into your center and see yourself glow from within. Through your center in the tree that you have created in your inner landscape, you can reach out and touch and tug on your auric egg, the outermost layer of your aura. Reaffirm your center

and let all the layers of your aura, your subtle bodies, move into harmony and alignment. Attend to whatever healing, respite, or work you need to do.

7. When the work is done, re-enter your inner landscape, release the tree visualization, and reconnect with the outer world. If you do nothing, it will also fade out on its own, but releasing it is better.

Notes

- If you have not worked with a personalized inner landscape, do so before using this method. It needs to be your place of power, not one borrowed from a guided visualization. It may reveal itself when you explore your inner reaches, or it may be partly something that you create and partly something that emerges on its own.
- If you work with the Four Elements, you may add them to step 3 as internal acknowledgments or calls. As another option, you may also wish to acknowledge your orientation in space as that which is before you, behind you, to your left, and to your right. Whatever system you use to organize and describe the macrocosm can be applied in this form of grounding and centering.
- If you don't work with one of the systems that uses the chakras or layers of the aura, then make sure you keep this form of grounding and centering anchored fully within yourself. Feel free to adapt it to your understanding of ethereal anatomy. The essence of this practice is recognizing yourself as a microcosm that is complete and whole unto itself.

Shielding

Perhaps the most common advice given to people who are experiencing a psychic overload or discomfort is to shield themselves. The first time I heard this advice, it conjured up images of starships raising their shields in a myriad of stories I'd read or watched. I had not had specific training about shielding, but the image in my mind was enough to begin the process. As with most things magickal, your power and your control start from your capacity to imagine. This is not make-believe; it is believe to make it real. By visualizing, realizing the shield, you are sending a message to the deeper parts of your psyche that know how to create the shield.

There are many types of shields, but most fall into one of two categories: modifications to one or more layers of your aura, or energetic projections. Changing the properties and behavior of your aura often comes more naturally, so it is how most people begin their efforts at shielding. With practice, our subtle bodies respond to our will and bidding as quickly as our physical bodies. Projecting energy outward from our subtle bodies so that it becomes separate from our subtle bodies but remains organized and under our guidance is more difficult.

The benefit of externalized projections that are mostly detached from the aura is that they provide real insulation from outside influences. They also have less of an impact when a shield fails. My experience has been that for most people, the changes made to their shields are only to their auric boundaries, even when they are trying for projections. Making projected shields takes practice and concerted effort because it requires raising, shaping, releasing, and placing energy outside the boundaries of your aura. Only a small tether or conduit connects the externalized shield with you in order to maintain and to control it. With repeated practice, it becomes possible to create a double shield composed of a modified aura and a projected shield.

The mirror, the wall, the net, and the glory are the four most common and effective types of shields. Their descriptive names are also the basic instructions for their creation. The power of your imagination governs both the creation and control of your shields. Each of these four can be envisioned many different ways, so really they are more like families of shield forms, rather than just four types. At first, regardless of your intention, these are likely to be modifications of the layers of your aura. With practice, you'll be able to do these as externalized or double shields.

Mirror Shield

To create a mirror shield, envision the outer layers of your aura becoming reflective so that anything impinging on it is deflected like light from a mirror. This sort of shield also makes it harder for others to sense and read you. You may wish to experiment with visualizing different kinds of reflective materials to find what works best for you. The essence of the mirror shield is the capacity to reflect. You may find it easier to envision polished metal or glossy white porcelain than a mirror. You can also vary the opacity of this shield so that it functions as a two-way mirror; in this way, your subtle senses are not blocked.

Wall Shield

To create a wall shield, envision the outer layers of your aura becoming a thick and solid wall. Some people visualize a brick or stone wall, but any type of wall that you associate with unyielding protection will do. The wall, or fortress shield, is much more sturdy than a mirror shield and is a very strong defense.

Unfortunately, this type of shield also makes it harder for you to perceive the energetic environment around you, and keeping it active requires more energy. The wall shield also reduces the amount of power you can draw in from outside yourself. In addition, others can more easily sense that you are shielded when you are using the wall shield.

Net Shield

To create a net shield, envision the outer layers of your aura becoming like a web of light with lines that keep out what is undesirable and openings that allow healthy energy to enter. In effect, you are asking your aura to behave like the semipermeable membranes that surround your cells that govern what can enter and exit. This is the template for creating the net shield. This versatile shield is useful in many settings because it protects without impeding perception. The strength of this shield is determined to a great degree by the integration of the practitioner's psyche, the whole of their levels and parts of soul, spirit, and consciousness. The net shield requires visualization, intention, and self-knowledge.

Glory Shield

The term *glory* in religious and spiritual art refers to the glow of a halo and aureola that encircles holy beings. To create a glory shield, envision the outer layers of your aura becoming radiant and shining with the purest light you can envision. This is the first type of shielding that I was taught, and when I teach classes on the topic, it is also the type that most of the students have encountered. It is often the only type of shielding that many people use. I coined the term *glory shield* to describe this form and to distinguish it from the other types of shielding.

The essence of this type of shield is self-identification with the power of light, the universe, the Divine, or whatever the person views as a source of life force and beneficence. The glory shield is very effective against unwholesome spirits, tainted places, negative workings, and the like. It does not do much to block strong emotions from other people or neutral or healthy spiritual energies whose high intensity can cause discomfort or damage.

There are many other types of shields, but you can address most situations with one of these four types. You can also combine shield types in creative ways to manage specific needs. For example, you may wish to create a shield wherein you envision a suit or mirror-bright armor. Or perhaps you'll create a shield that is a fortress with brilliance at its center that is a holy sanctuary. The possibilities are nearly endless, bounded only by your skill and creativity. Shields that are a combination of types are easier to create as externalized constructs rather than as modifications of the aura.

Five Fingers: A Procedure for Managing Overloads

When a person is being subjected to a psychic overload and/or to toxic energies, calmly analyzing the source of the discomfort is difficult. The greater the discomfort, the greater the tendency to shy away from examining the source of the problem. The *Five Fingers* is a step-by-step process that breaks the process of analyzing and addressing an overload into manageable chunks. The goal of this practice is to become aware of the situation and then to take as much control of your reactions and of the situation as is possible and reasonable.

When I teach this procedure, I usually get a number of questions that fall into the "Are we there yet?" category. The desire for a quick fix is understandable, but a real resolution to the problem requires adherence to the whole process. Before you choose a solution, it is important to understand what is occurring. I use the five fingers of the hand as a memory device, a mnemonic, to help in remembering the five steps when experiencing the stress of a psychic overload. I've provided an illustration to help you commit the Five Fingers to your memory.

Pinky Finger: Check Environment

The first step is to become aware of your current environment. Take stock of who and what are present, both seen and unseen. Ask yourself what you know of the history, circumstances, and current situation. What is the spiritual history or reputation of the place and/or the beings that are present? Use your physical and subtle senses to take brief and careful observations of your surroundings. Begin to form a reasoned and logical understanding of the context of what you are experiencing. If you need an image to remind you of what the pinky finger represents, think of lifting your pinky into the air to test the direction of the wind.

Ring Finger: Whose Feelings?

The second step is to distinguish between your feelings and sensations and those that you are absorbing from the environment. What were your physical sensations and feelings immediately before you came in contact with the environment that you find troubling? How and when did those sensations and feelings change? Is there a logical reason for you to be having these reactions and this level of intensity? Whenever it is feasible, remove yourself from the environment and then re-enter to compare the differences in your perceptions. If you need an image to remind you of what the ring finger represents, think of the old story that the ring finger connects to the heart and as such is chosen for wedding rings.

Middle Finger: Ground to Yourself

The third step is to use the "grounding and centering to yourself" method that I described earlier in this chapter. Doing this work in your inner landscape enables you to process what you have established in the first two steps in a mind-space that shelters you from the outer influences. You can also take refuge in this space so that you can recover enough to take action in the next two steps. If you need an image to remind you of what the middle finger represents, take note that it is the tallest finger, the center finger, and is the tree.

Index Finger: Point and Block

In the fourth step, you begin to take action to manage the overload by tackling whatever you've identified as the strongest source of discomfort. I am fairly certain that at some time you've blotted out the glare of the Sun with your fingertips. With the glare blocked, sight is no longer painful, and you can see your surroundings more clearly. To do this, you create a shield that just blocks the source of the greatest discomfort. Most of the time, this will be a small shield that does not enclose your entire aura. By envisioning a small shield, like a buckler, you are creating a nimble shield that moves and adjusts to the need at hand. In more extreme cases, you can have full aura shields and a small active shield. Another option is to envision that your aura becomes reflective or opaque wherever the energy impact is the strongest. Think of this as acting in a similar fashion to prescription glasses that darken in bright light. If you need an image to remind you of what the index finger represents, just think of pointing a finger to block the glare, and also the pentacle shield.

Thumb: A Proactive Grip

In the fifth step, you pull it all together and get a grip on the situation. In addition to whatever shielding choices you make, you usually reframe the situation to make it more psychologically manageable. All the psychological tricks that work with pain management can also be applied to the discomfort of a psychic overload. It is about choosing your stance and your relationship to your encounter with the circumstances. It is also valuable to regain perspective on how long the disagreeable intensity will last. It has a limited duration, and steeling yourself with that knowledge can grant you endurance. A sense of choice and control goes a long way to making any scenario more manageable.

You may discover that with the composure you've achieved by the time you reach this step, other options become available to you. One of them is to equalize the pressure exerted by your aura with that of your environment. If you've flown on a plane, you may have felt the difference in pressure between the air in the cabin with the pressure in your ears. This discomfort is usually resolved by moving your jaw, yawning, or chewing gum until you feel the pop that means that the pressure inside of you is in equilibrium with the pressure outside of you. Similarly, by pulling in or pushing out your aura, you can reach equilibrium with your environment and reduce discomfort. If you need an image to remind you of what the thumb represents, just think of the thumb as being capable of touching all the fingers. The thumb activates the whole hand, thus the symbol of the hand.

CHAPTER 6

The Eternal Now Exercise

> *If the doors of perception were cleansed every thing would appear to man as it is, infinite. For man has closed himself up, till he sees all things thro' narrow chinks of his cavern.*
>
> —William Blake from *The Marriage of Heaven and Hell*

Introduction

Many often hope that if they open the doors of the Lower Self and of psychic perception, they will gain a full vision and knowledge of the greater reality that surrounds them. While it is true enough that this will bring about experiences, and perhaps coax the seeker through one of the openings in their Platonic cavern, it is not enough to cleanse the doors of perception. To have some chance of accomplishing this feat requires the skill of the Middle Self joined with the counsel of the Higher Self. The Higher Self recognizes what is perceived by understanding essential natures and webs of interconnection that surpass the causal. As such, the Higher Self contains wisdom that is beyond the knowledge of the Middle Self or the vital instinct of the Lower Self. The Higher Self is the part of us that is closest to the infinite and as such can see the infinite in things with greater clarity. The Higher Self has the capacity to make sense of what is perceived in the subtle realms.

While we are incarnate, there are three common methods to commune with the Higher Self. One is to have your center of consciousness descend into the Lower Self, which more openly welcomes that influence of the Higher Self that reaches down to embrace the younger self. This is the most common approach because it is the easiest. It does allow the Higher Self to guide our actions and perceptions to some degree, but does not result in a refinement or an integration of the three Selves.

The second approach is to prepare a way for the Higher Self to descend into the Middle Self through self-awareness of our motives, needs, and personality structures. This approach requires more time and repeated efforts to remove the resistance created by unhealthy expressions of ego. Ultimately, it results in evolutionary changes that help to bring will and Higher Will into concordance.

The third way is the way of the mystic and devotional practice, wherein the goal is to raise the center of consciousness to the level of the Higher Self. This approach can lead to flashes of transcendent comprehension of the world, but often without a path to apply those insights to the world that we live in.

I have developed an exercise that I call the *invocation of the eternal now* that takes a different approach to support spiritual refinement through the joining of the three Selves. It works by bringing more of the Higher Self and the Lower Self into the awareness of the Middle Self at the place where the three touch in the eternal now. By the eternal now, I mean the place where the now of linear time intersects with all the points in time that are nonlinear, but are synchronistically linked to the moment of perception. The eternal now is the moment that also takes into consideration the momentum of time.

This exercise requires a fairly strenuous use of your visualization skills, which some may find daunting at first. Building the mental forms in this exercise is easier than you would guess because the forms are linked to underlying constructs that will uphold your efforts. I use the word *exercise* because your success at this work will improve with repetition. You may receive some immediate benefit, but real progress will require regular practice of this exercise. The complexity of the sigil used in the invocation of the greater now is what engages the Middle Self mind sufficiently so that it opens itself to the Higher Self.

One of the differences between the Middle Self and the Higher Self is how time is experienced. The Middle Self's default framework is that of linear time, in which time flows like a river. The Higher Self's default framework is that of eternal time, in which time flows with the tides, currents, waves, and eddies of an ocean. The multidimensional sigil, which is the foundation of this exercise, modulates the density of time within the person's frame of reference. Time density is the core parameter that distinguishes linear time from eternity. Think of time as a medium and a matrix. When time is as thin as the air that surrounds you, it is possible to walk through it with very little effort in the direction of your choice. It takes a very strong wind to prevent you from moving backward or forward or sideways. This is time in the higher planes. When time is a rushing river, you may be able to hold your own against the current for a bit, but swimming upstream is not feasible. This is time in the lower planes. In the physical plane, the current of time is so dense that we cannot resist it and are carried forward.

Invocation of the Eternal Now

A quiet room with low lighting is useful for this exercise. Make sure you have turned off your phone or any other device that might startle you with a notification. Have a pad or a journal ready because you will want to write about the experience when you are done. The first several times that you do this exercise, you may wish to keep this book handy as a reference for the steps in the exercise.

1. Create three spheres of blue-green energy, as shown in the diagram, aligned to the vertical axis of your body. The top of the upper sphere should touch the top of your head. The bottom of the lower sphere should touch the soles of your feet. The middle sphere is in your core with the center over your Root Chakra. The upper and the lower sphere should intersect in the middle sphere so that they touch at the point that is the center of the middle sphere.

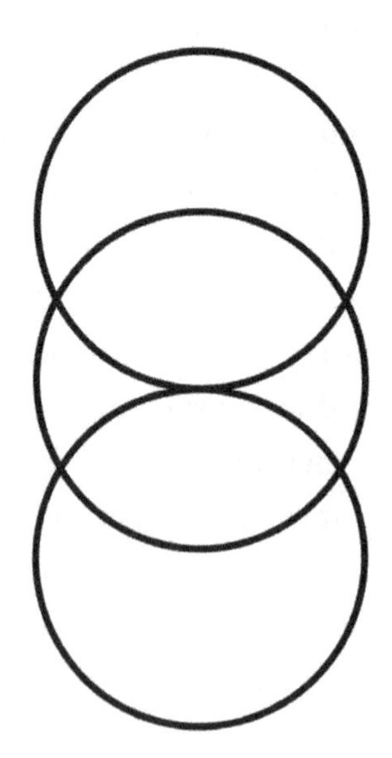

2. Blue-green is the range of color that corresponds to the midpoint and intersection of those energies that are fully Pranic (organic) and those energies that are fully Elemental. The three spheres represent the Lower, Middle, and Higher Selves and all their correlations, such as the Lower, Middle, and Upper Worlds. This is a symbolic representation, so the exact positioning of the spheres is not critical. Two considerations are necessary in this visualization. One is that the top of the upper sphere must reach to the top of your Crown Chakra and that the lower sphere should touch the soles of your feet with the bottom of the sphere being centered beneath you. The second consideration is that the upper and lower spheres should intersect the middle sphere so that where they touch each other is also the center point of the middle sphere. You may do this standing, sitting, or flat on your back so long as these relationships are preserved.
3. Create an octahedron that surrounds the middle sphere using blue-green energy. The octahedron should be bright, crisp, and distinct against the spheres. Four of the vertices of the octahedron should extend outside your body. Two vertices should be aligned to your vertical axis, your spine. The octahedron represents the seven sacred directions of the four compass points, the above, the below, and the center. When you bring the octahedron into being, you should also call into awareness your understanding of the four elements as well as the flow of energy that is your central column, your middle pillar. The octahedron should be big enough so that it just barely encloses the central sphere. You can substitute a cube for the octahedron, but most people find it harder to visualize the cube properly.

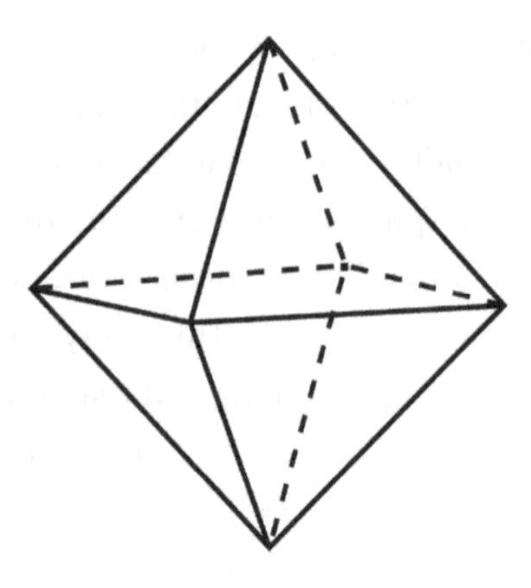

4. Create two tetrahedrons whose vertices touch in the center of the Central Sphere using blue-green energy. Tetrahedrons are a form of pyramid that has four sides, all of which are triangles. In this sigil construct, the tetrahedron represents the triadic principles such as cardinal, fixed, and mutable; past, present, and future; salt, sulfur, and mercury; and many more. These principles are the next order of principles above that of the four-fold pattern that includes the Elements. There are two tetrahedrons, one pointing up and one pointing down with one point of connection. This is a depiction of the upward flow and the downward flow that is the cycle of spirit and matter.

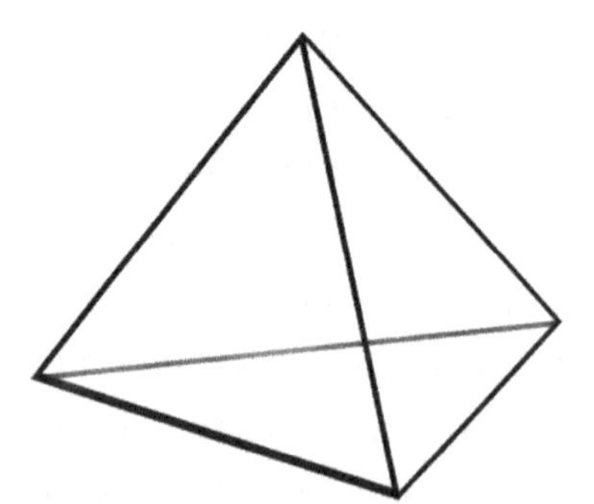

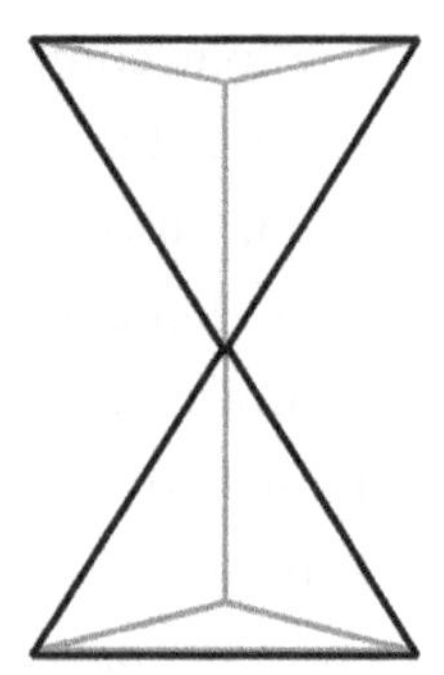

5. Put the two tetrahedrons in motion so that they spin so fast that they look like two cones. To begin the process of spinning the tetrahedrons, focus your attention on your center, which is also the centerpoint of this sigil construct. Feel a gentle swirling motion in your center and let it grow stronger. Then transfer the motion to the tetrahedrons. The faster the tetrahedrons spin, the stronger the effect. If they spin counter to each other, it is more effective but initially harder to visualize. When the tetrahedrons are spinning at full speed, they should blur and resemble two cones, two vortices.

6. The spinning of the tetrahedrons represents the interplay between immanence and transcendence, whose outgrowth is what we call time. The faster they spin, the broader our sense of the now. Our sense of time is expanded from the fleeting dot that is the mundane present to ever larger circles of an expanded now of mystic awareness. In effect, we move from a denser to a more subtle flow and field of time.

7. Proceed with meditations, contemplations, communications, and observations. Should you feel that your consciousness is drifting back toward normal waking consciousness, gently refresh your visualization of the sigil. When you are finished, take time to consciously move your insights into your memories. It is also valuable to record these exercises in a journal as another way to anchor the work within yourself. You should do this before dismissing the invocation of the greater now.

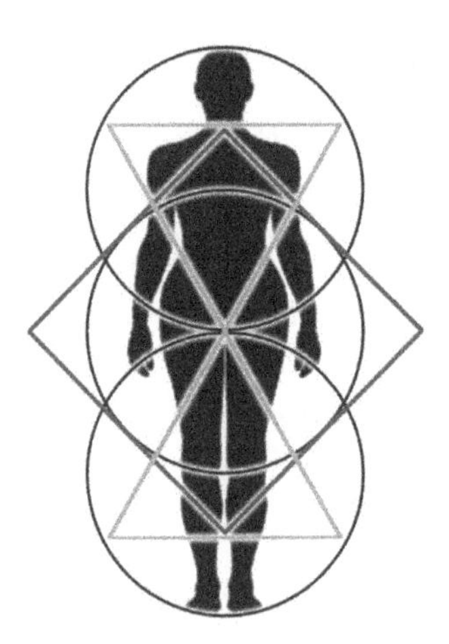

8. To dismiss this working, first stop the motion of the tetrahedrons; then drain the color away until the forms are faint outlines and let them fade. See them fade like soap bubbles whose colors swirl and pale before they pop. Take some time for your energy to settle back to normal before doing anything else.

Suggestions

The first few times that you use this exercise, simply spend time within it without a task in mind. Once you are accustomed to the changes to your consciousness, then proceed with a goal or task in mind. For example, try to do a reading using your preferred method—tarot, runes, and so on—while in the greater now. Another possibility is to experiment with seeing and understanding the patterns in another person's aura. If you do psychometry, reading the history of an object by touching it, you may find that you sense more details and more context for the information you receive while doing this exercise. When you have gained comfort and confidence in using this exercise, you may want to try to experience a ritual or a working while in this state of consciousness. Also, don't underestimate the value of simply doing the exercise just for the sake of encouraging more unity among your three Selves. This, in and of itself, will refine your perceptions and understanding of the subtle realms.

CHAPTER 7

The Bridge of Fire and Water: A Ritual for Speaking for Spirits

Introduction

Early in my development as a magical practitioner, I was trained in mediumship and channeling by teachers outside the Pagan community. Over the course of time, I created my own methods for mediumship, channeling, and meditation that incorporated teachings from my Pagan and magickal training into what I'd learned from other communities. One of the methods I'd like to share is a ritual that I finished polishing in the mid-1990s; I call it the *Bridge of Fire and Water*. This ritual tends to produce clear and lucid communications but is intended for people who have already been trained and are working as mediums or oracles, or are using related practices. It is not very effective for neophytes, but if you have some sort of magickal training in trance and energy management, that may be enough to make this ritual/method work for you. In addition to the virtue of clarity of communication, I find that I can stay focused longer, with fewer lingering effects, using this ritual than using other methods. The longest I stayed in lucid contact with a single spirit using this method was just under two hours; the normal working time is closer to one hour. Depending on the nature of the spirit that is being contacted and the spirit's location in space-time, the speaker for the spirit may or may not have a clear memory of what they say in the session. It works best for communicating with the spirits that have been physically incarnated at some point, the human dead in particular. It can be used with other sorts of beings such as God/dess/es, fae, angels, and so on, if the person acting as the speaker has worked with them in other contexts. Only one specific spirit should be called per session with this ritual. This is not the ritual to use if you intend to do multiple short audiences with spirits.

This ritual uses the power of the Elements of Fire and Water to create a bridge between the consciousness of the spirit and the consciousness of the speaker. If you are uncertain of your knowledge and familiarity with the Four Elements model in magick, please do a bit of research before attempting this ritual. The power of the Elements of Fire and Water are not just invoked, but are anchored into physical fire and water. The physical water in this rite should be enlivened and be seen as the primal Water, the universal solvent, and the mirror of *Briah*. The physical fire in this rite should be enlivened and be seen as the primal Fire, the electric fire, and the light of *Atziluth*.

To be sure that there is no misunderstanding, let me explain what I mean by enlivening the physical water and the fire used in this ritual. Just as we have physical bodies that have souls and are connected to a higher spiritual source, the physical elements also have a connection to the higher elemental powers, the spirit of their Element. To enliven the water in a bowl or the flame of a candle, we use our words, energy, and visualization to draw down their corresponding higher elemental powers. You may think of it as asking the water and the flame to become mediums, channels, vessels, and anchors for the power of the Elements. The physical elements in isolation, like a bowl of water or candle flame, lack the will and power to awaken themselves to their spiritual source. When we enliven them for ritual use, that is what we are doing.

Props and Setup

You will need three small tables or pedestals, a bowl of cold water, and two large candles, ideally in glass. The water should be fresh and clear. River water is best, but, if unavailable, tap water from a faucet is fine. Many people use a bit of salt in their ritual water, but, in this case, it would interfere with the ritual, so please refrain from adding any salt. However, a few drops of the cologne Kananga Water in the bowl is helpful. Alternatively, add a drop or two of the essential oil of ylang ylang (*Cananga odorata*), which is the key ingredient in Kananga Water.

A chair is placed in the center of the ritual space. A lit candle is placed to the right and another lit candle to the left of the chair on small tables or pedestals. The candles are set so that they are visible within the edge of the peripheral vision of the person who will sit in the chair and be the voice for the Spirits. The person should be able to easily reach out and touch the candles. My preference is for either white or black candles, but you may use whatever color works for you. I do suggest that both candles be the same height and color to avoid distractions. A small table or pedestal with a bowl of cold water is placed in front of the chair where the speaker will sit. The bowl should be large enough and close enough so that most of the speaker's hands can be submerged in the water. If possible, the light of the candles should be reflected in the water.

This ritual works equally well whether it is done during the day or the night. It is better if the lighting in the room is dim, and the room has been soundproofed enough to minimize extraneous noises. Have a few glasses of water handy in case someone begins to cough or clear their throat. The participants should be seated during the ritual, to minimize any distress that can arise from standing for a long period of time. The goal is to keep the energy in the space quiet on all the planes. Once the ritual starts, no one may enter or exit. Make sure that this ritual takes place in a space where interruptions can be prevented. The ground rules and expectations for the participants should be announced before the ritual begins.

Beginning

Even if you are working in a consecrated place and are unconcerned about spiritual or energetic intrusions, a casting is needed to focus the energy and the information that moves through this ritual. Casting a circle is the simplest and most direct approach, and many styles and systems could be used to good effect. Instructions for casting circles are readily available. Some systems and traditions do not use this kind of ritual container, and if you are tempted to skip it because you think this is just a liturgical whim, you are mistaken. If you feel compelled to avoid casting a circle, then come up with a substitute that fits your practices that acts as an energetic vessel, invites the support of the Divine, and protects the speaker who will be in a vulnerable state during the ritual. Ideally, the person who casts the circle should not be the person who will have the role of the speaker. I have offered this ritual without helpers, and while it can be done, it is not advisable. A better scenario is one in which there is a separate caster who can also act as the warder if that becomes necessary. A warder, in this context, is a person who monitors the spiritual and physical state of the speaker, is on guard against unwholesome presences, and knows how to intervene when necessary.

The best-case scenario is one in which you have a speaker, a caster, a warder, and a scribe. If you have a scribe, that person's function is to write down the session as it runs, and if you have no objection, to monitor a recording device to capture the whole session while taking notes. There have been times when the recordings have patches of static and other noises that have made the written notes very important.

After the circle is cast, all those present chant "Endless Eternal." While the chanting is going on, the speaker disconnects the energetic linkage between their feet and the Earth. The speaker must become intentionally ungrounded. Then they re-anchor themselves to their solar plexus, their Lower Self, their *Guph/Nephesh* mind, and their animal self. The speaker moves their center of consciousness to their Throat Chakra. The speaker should then draw the subtle fire from each candle to form a veil of fire that stretches from candle to candle and fills their field of vision. The veil of fire should curve inward so that it touches some layer of their Throat Chakra. Then the speaker should place their fingers in the bowl of water and await the next step. This is the chant that I use:

Endless Eternal, Powers of the Night
Endless Eternal, Powers of the Day
Endless Eternal, by Dusk and by Dawn
Come to Us Now, Come to Us Now
We Who Live in Time, We Who Live and Die
We Who Live in Time, We Who Cross the Veil

We Who Live in Time, Are Here and Are There

Flow through Us Now, Flow through Us Now

You may listen to an MP3 of this chant at *www.ivodominguezjr.com/Panpipes_Pagan_Chant_Site/chants/EndlessEternal.html.*

If you have an appropriate chant or song that you use in your traditions, you may use it instead of my chant. It is important that it be a chant or song that can be sung by a significant percentage of the attendees. In addition to offering support to the speaker, chanting together makes the group's energy more coherent and interconnected.

The caster (preferably) should then name the person/spirit that is being sought in the ritual. When possible, the name should be repeated aloud several times and augmented by details of the person's life or the spirit's epithets and characteristics at each repetition. This naming should be spoken loudly and clearly over the chanting. The chanting continues softly until the speaker is ready. Only one spirit may be sought per ritual. If you attempt to contact multiple spirits, this ritual will become exhausting, and there is an increase in the risk of an interloping spirit. Occasionally, the spirit you contact will bring another through the portal of their selfhood, but that is initiated by them, not you. The speaker should feel through the water and seek a connection. For me, this feeling and seeking involve both a physical movement of my fingers combined with the image and sense of my hands being vast and each small movement crossing time and space. When the connection is made and verified as being the right one, let the spirit flow up the fingers, the arms, and into the Throat Chakra.

There is no simple litmus to confirm the identity of the spirit, but loading your mind with a template of the shape of the spirit that is sought does help. Collecting information and any available myth or lore or life history is the first step. Gazing on images that represent the spirit that you can hold in your mind's eye is the next step. Depending on the spirit that is sought, this could be anything from family photos to pictures of sacred sites, to statues, to religious iconography, and so on. The work to prepare to familiarize yourself with the spirit must occur before the ritual—preferably hours or days before the working so that there is time for the information to sink deeper into your psyche.

The speaker announces when they are ready to take questions. Sometimes the speaker merely lifts their head and looks at those gathered in the ritual. Occasionally, the caster may have to intervene and ask the speaker if they are ready. This is done if the speaker has lost track of linear time within their internal process. Ideally, the caster, or warder, has the skill, senses, and experience to discern if that is the case. If it is taking a long time for the speaker to connect with the spirit, the chanting should gently be brought to a close, followed by soft toning of AUM, and then silence until the speaker is ready. It is uncommon, but if the connection does not feel solid or a warning is given by the spirit, the speaker should announce that the ritual must be ended. Another attempt can be done on another day or night.

Middle

The speaker may need to adjust the position of their fingers in the water to maintain the connection several times over the course of the ritual session. The physical motion of the fingers helps to keep the connection flowing through the Lower Self, the dreaming self. The veil of fire drawn between the two candles will keep the Throat Chakra energized and warded so that the spirit does not move further into the speaker than it should. The speaker should be mindful of their bodily sensations for signals indicating when they need to disconnect from the spirit contact. This rite works well at extending the period of time the speaker can stay in trance, but it still takes an expenditure of energy that is taxing. If multiple people are asking questions, the caster or another person should be chosen to keep the questioning orderly. The caster and the group as a whole should be mindful of the state of the speaker because the speaker doesn't always know when to stop.

I advise against any efforts to send energetic support to the speaker, as it tends to be disruptive of both the contact and the speaker's aura. If the participants want to be of service, the best option is to remain focused and quiet. Participants should not ask questions that do not pertain to the field of knowledge of the spirit that has been called.

Ending

To begin to end the rite, the speaker should brighten their Throat Chakra, draw in the subtle fire of the veil, and push the spirit down their arms and back into the water and release it. They should remove their fingers from the bowl of water while continuing to push subtle fire through their fingertips. Then the subtle fire should be used to cleanse the Throat Chakra first, then flushed through the whole body so that the entire aura glows brightly. This cleansing is to remove the echo and imprint of the spirit. Then the speaker should ground and reconnect their feet to the Earth. Their center of consciousness should be returned to whatever energy center/chakra location is their norm. Then the veil of fire is pushed back into the candles. The speaker should briefly hold their palms over the flames and seal the minor chakras in their palms. Sometimes it is necessary to have the caster or warder talk the speaker through the steps to end the session. It is also wise to keep some Florida Water handy; it can be used to anoint the throat and the nape of the neck of the speaker. If the candles are still lit, be careful because Florida Water is flammable.

The caster should ensure that the speaker is clear and present. The caster should ask the speaker to say their own name aloud and, if needed, to answer a few simple questions about themselves. The caster should thank and formally dismiss the spirit to ensure that it is not lingering in the space. The candles should be extinguished. The circle should be dismissed and opened. The water from the bowl should be poured outside or down the drain, but should not be offered as a libation or kept for future use. The bowl should be cleaned and dried soon after the ritual. The candles may be reused at another session, if enough of the candles is left.

Aftercare

The speaker may be unsteady on their feet, so make sure that they are physically safe. Keep an eye on the speaker, as the full impact of the ritual work may not become apparent until minutes or even hours later. The speaker will often want to gorge after the work, often on chocolate or sweets. They should have water and something with protein, and some sweets if they desire, but all in moderation. A bit of alcohol is fine if that is their custom. If the speaker does not feel hungry, press the need for a drink of juice, tea, coffee, or whatever beverage normally appeals to them. After they drink, it is often easier to encourage a bite of something solid. Also, they may be too warm or too cold, depending on their nature, and may need a cooling drink or a blanket. If the speaker wants to talk about their experience of the ritual, that is fine, but discourage the other participants from posing questions. Questioning may pull the person back into a contact with the spirit without the benefit of the ritual structure and without time for recuperation.

CHAPTER 8

A Variation on the Middle Pillar Ritual

Introduction

When Israel Regardie's book *The Middle Pillar* was published in 1938, he gave the world access to important materials that had hitherto been available only to members of certain magickal orders. Contained in the book was the *Middle Pillar Ritual,* which over the decades has become one of the cornerstones of magickal practice in a wide range of traditions. Regardie had learned an early form of the Middle Pillar Ritual from Dr. Robert Felkin while he was a member of Stella Matutina, an offshoot of the Golden Dawn. The form that he shares in *The Middle Pillar* was Regardie's modified and, in my opinion, improved version of the ritual. I strongly encourage you to pick up a copy of *The Middle Pillar* if you are unfamiliar with this material. A wide range of articles on this topic is available through the Internet. The ritual draws its symbolic structure from the Tree of Life and works to place the participant in a balanced connection to the circuit of power that courses through from the infinite to the finite and back again. It encourages the manifestation of your

Divine Self, your God-Self, by blending your light with Divine light. The Middle Pillar Ritual is one of the best tools for those who are engaged in the Great Work of conscious evolution.

The Middle Pillar Ritual is a two-part ritual. The first part is the awakening of the correlates of the Spheres of the Middle Pillar on the vertical axis of the person. The second part involves the circulation of light through the body in one of three modes that parallels the descent and return of energy on the Tree of Life. The two parts together represent states of being and states of process, the reflective and the active, that together call forth the third state that is closer to illumination, light in extension. Although the Middle Pillar Ritual can be used as a stand-alone working, it is often used as a component of a sequence of workings or rituals.

For those of you who are not students of the Qabala, this may seem a bit confusing. The Qabala, the Tree of Life, is a summation of the forces and patterns that make up the Microcosm, the Mesocosm, and the Macrocosm. It is the symbol of wholeness for manifest creation. It is the grammar, dialectic, and rhetoric that prepare the student for the subject of the Great Work. The Middle Pillar of the Tree is the place where the work of creating synthesis, balance, and integration occurs. Middle Pillar–inspired rituals support the work of bringing all the Selves into alignment.

I have created a variation on the Middle Pillar Ritual whose purpose is to bring more of the Higher Self, Divine Spark, God-Self, whatever term you prefer, into the awareness of your conscious mind. I have had a number of students that were not well suited for the traditional Middle Pillar Ritual because of their powerful sensitivity to shifts in energy and consciousness. In some cases, they needed more time and practice, and in others, they were simply not compatible with the ritual itself. Even the most trusted and revered rituals are not safe and effective for everyone. If you find that you run into a traditional ritual, such as the Middle Pillar Ritual or any other, that does not sit well with you, then give it your concerted efforts several times. Should you find that despite your best work it never *clicks in*, do not assume that you failed and were found lacking. You may just need a different approach.

I was motivated to create a variation on the Middle Pillar Ritual that did not directly channel the energy of working through the aura, energy bodies, of the ritualist. The fortuitous outcome of this effort was that I created a ritual that is good for the needs of my sensitive students, and is better at creating conscious awareness of the Divine Spark than the original ritual for most people who have tried it. As is true of all Middle Pillar Rituals, the more you know about the Tree of Life, the better it will work. However, I have conducted my variation, which I call the *Middle Pillar Circle*, with people who had no background in the Qabala, and they reported that it worked for them. I do encourage you to study the Qabala because it is the foundation of most of the magickal and divinatory systems in the West. You don't have to wait until you know more about the Qabala to try my Middle Pillar Circle. The powers and the patterns that are called forth in the ritual respond well enough so long as there is a sincere effort to commit to the ritual.

The Middle Pillar Circle

1) Purification

Begin with a simple purification before starting the ritual. Dip your fingers into salt water that you have blessed with the powers of the Elements of Water and Earth. As you dip your fingers, feel your worries flow into the salt water. Bless and light whatever incense you prefer, to represent the powers of the Elements of Fire and Air. Use your hands to waft smoke over your head and let the incense bring you inspiration and carry forth your intentions. Lastly, use a mirror to look into your own eyes to find the Divine spark within yourself.

2) Middle Pillar Circle Casting

The casting, the container, for this ritual follows the well-established pattern of calling and anchoring powers and presences at the Four Directions. Instead of the Four Elements, Archangels, or the like, we call upon the Spheres on the Tree of Life and their associated planetary powers at the Four Directions. Symbolically, the Middle Pillar is turned round into a circle so that Kether and Malkuth meet.

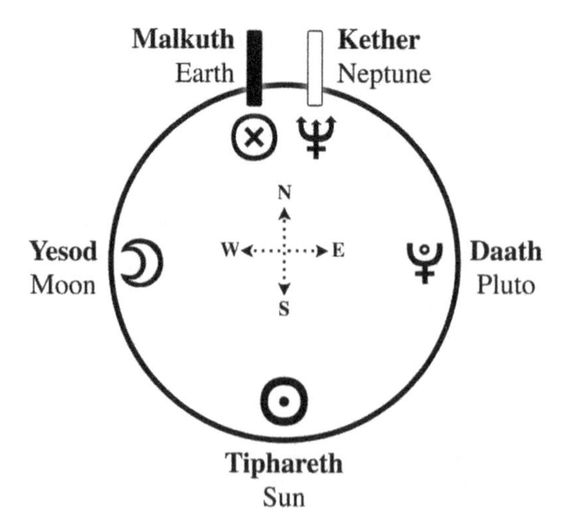

It is possible to do this ritual with no props at all or with a full array of props and altars. If you are a student of the Qabala or the Western Magickal Tradition, you have an abundance of options for dressing the altars of the Spheres and Planets. If you are not plugged into these systems, the invocations that I share in this chapter will be enough. Even if your tastes or needs are minimalist, at the very least consider a black and a white candle in the North to represent the place where Heaven and Earth meet. You can modify this ritual to work in a small room where you just turn in place or in a larger space where you move from altar to altar.

After purification, go to the north and to the white candle or pillar that represents Kether. Slowly take several deep breaths and close your eyes. Find within yourself the bright power of your soul and spirit. Hold both of your hands palms up and say:

I call to the vast expanse of Neptune that is the source of all beginnings.

I call to the First Light, ineffable brilliance that shines upon all that can be.

I awaken to Kether.

Then, using the index finger of your stronger hand, scribe a clockwise spiral of white energy in front of you. Start the spiral in the center and move outward. Take a moment to acknowledge the presence and the power, and then move clockwise to the eastern altar.

Slowly take several deep breaths and close your eyes. Find within yourself the liminal places, the thresholds, the boundaries of knowing, of your soul and spirit. Hold both of your hands palms up and say:

I call to the abyss of Pluto where things are undone to become.

I call to the Hidden Light, that knows what it cannot know.

I awaken to Daath.

Then using the index finger of your stronger hand, scribe a clockwise spiral of lavender energy in front of you. Start the spiral in the center and move outward. Take a moment to acknowledge the presence and the power, and then move clockwise to the southern altar.

Slowly take several deep breaths and close your eyes. Find within yourself the balance point, where harmony and equilibrium are found in your soul and spirit. Hold both of your hands palms up and say:

I call to the Central Sun, that gives of itself to enliven all beings.

I call to the Beautiful Light, that brings order and purpose.

I awaken to Tiphereth.

Then, using the index finger of your stronger hand, scribe a clockwise spiral of yellow energy in front of you. Start the spiral in the center and move outward. Take a moment to acknowledge the presence and the power, and then move clockwise to the western altar.

Slowly take several deep breaths and close your eyes. Find within yourself the place of flux and foundation that is deep within your soul and spirit. Hold both of your hands palms up and say:

I call to the Moon that dwells in the seen and unseen.

I call to the Shaping Light, that gives birth to the world.

I awaken to Yesod.

Then, using the index finger of your stronger hand, scribe a clockwise spiral of violet energy in front of you. Start the spiral in the center and move outward. Take a moment to acknowledge the presence and the power, and then move clockwise and return the northern altar.

Slowly take several deep breaths and close your eyes. Find within yourself your grounding to the Earth and your soul and spirit's connection to the web of life. Facing the black candle or pillar that represents Malkuth, hold both of your hands palms up and say:

I call to Earth that is both womb and tomb of the manifest.

I call to the Queen of Light, that sits upon the throne of the world.

I awaken to Malkuth.

Then, using the index finger of your stronger hand, scribe a clockwise spiral of energy that is a braid of russet, olive green, yellow ochre, and black in front of you. Start the spiral in the center and move outward. Take a moment to acknowledge the presence and the power. Then take several deep breaths and draw in power for the next step.

Hold up your hands, one aligned with Malkuth and the other with Kether, and slowly bring your hands together, envisioning a veil of rainbow fire that closes the gap between the two. While doing this, say:

Let the Above and the Below be joined.

Kether is in Malkuth and Malkuth in Kether.

Then return to the center of the ritual space.

3) We Awaken the Pillar Within

Now we awaken the chakras and the central column of energy that aligns with the spine. This is done through toning and color visualization. If you are not familiar with one of the many systems to describe these structures within the subtle bodies, the instructions here will suffice for this purpose. I do recommend that you add the chakras to your studies if you have not already done so. The diagram shows the colors, sounds, and general locations for what you will visualize and intone in this ritual.

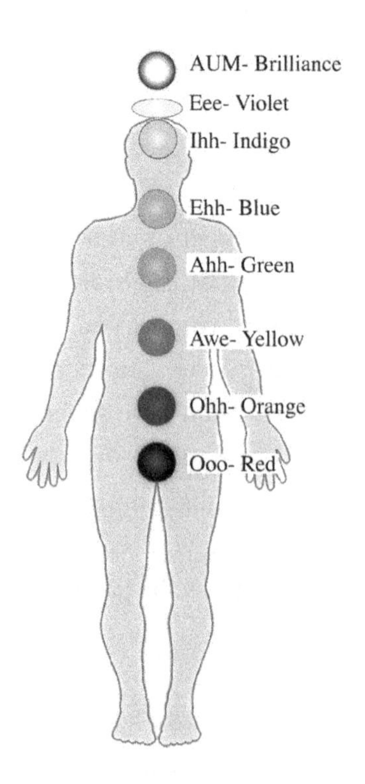

It is preferable to do this procedure standing, but you may sit in a chair if necessary. If you are seated, make sure that your legs are uncrossed with your feet flat on the ground. In either case, please face north toward the two pillars.

Envision the color red, first at the location of the lowest chakra at the base of the spine, and then filling your whole body with red. Intone the sound "Ooo" with a note as low as you can comfortably produce three times. Now move your awareness upward.

Envision the color orange, first at the location of the second chakra and then filling your whole body with orange. The second chakra is above the pubic bone and below the navel. Intone the sound "Ohh" with a note that is one step up from the previous note. Repeat this tone three times. Now move your awareness upward.

Envision the color yellow, first at the location of the third chakra and then filling your whole body with yellow. The third chakra is above the navel, below where the ribs join, in your solar plexus. Intone the sound "Awe" with a note one step up from the previous note. Once again, do this three times. Now move your awareness upward.

Envision the color green, first at the location of the fourth chakra and then filling your whole body with green. The fourth chakra is in the center of your chest between your breasts. Intone the sound "Ahh" with a note that is one step up from the previous note. Repeat this tone three times. Now move your awareness upward.

Envision the color blue, first at the location of the fifth chakra and then filling your whole body with blue. The fifth chakra is in the throat where your larynx is located. This should be the blue of the sky. Intone the sound "Ehh" with a note that is one step up from the previous note. You may feel a change in where you feel your voice resonate in your body. Repeat this tone three times. Now move your awareness upward.

Envision the color indigo, first at the location of the sixth chakra and then filling your whole body with indigo. The sixth chakra is on your brow in the classic location for the Third Eye.

This color is midway between blue and violet and is like the classic color of new blue jeans. Intone the sound "Ihh" with a note that is one step up from the previous note. Repeat this tone three times. Now move your awareness upward to the top of your head.

Envision the color violet, first at the location of the seventh chakra and then filling your whole body with violet. The seventh chakra is on the top of your head where the fontanelle, the soft spot in a baby's head, was when you were an infant. Intone the sound "Eee" with a note that is one step up from the previous note. You may feel this one vibrate strongly in your head. Repeat this tone three times. Now move your awareness about a fist's height above your head.

Envision the color white, a mixture of all colors, of brilliance, in a sphere floating above your head. Intone the sound "Aum" at whatever pitch feels best to you. See the light from the sphere flowing down over your body and then rising up through your spine. Repeat the toning and the visualization three times. Then take three deep breaths and pause before beginning the next step.

4) Awakening the Higher Mind

Walk the perimeter of the circle, and bow to each direction, beginning and ending in the north. Then chant:

As Above so Below Spirit and Matter

In a Dance so Slow

As Within so Without Great Mystery

That Spirals In and Out

Secret Glory, Hidden by Nothing

Thrice Blessed, Thrice Called, Thrice Revealed (2x)

You may listen to the chant here: *www.ivodominguezjr.com/Panpipes_Pagan_Chant_Site/chants/great-mystery.html.*

It is better if you chant, but if for whatever reason you cannot, recite these words as an invocation.

5) Opening to and Listening for Guidance

Sit or stand in the center of the circle. Drone/intone this prayer until it feels right to move into silent meditation. Periodically, take an energized breath and blow it upward.

I Am the Above, I Am the Below

I Am the Tree of My Life

I Am the Past, I Am the Future

I Am the Eternal Now

When you have received whatever you will receive from this ritual, end the silence with a punctuating sound such as a clap, bell, or rattle.

6) Ending the Ritual

Go to Malkuth's northern altar and say:

I give thanks to the power and the presence of Malkuth.

See the veil of rainbow fire that joins Malkuth and Kether flicker, fade, and be gone. Then, using the index finger of your stronger hand, scribe a counterclockwise spiral of energy that is a braid of russet, olive green, yellow ochre, and black in front of you. Start the spiral at the outer edge and move inward to the center.

Move counterclockwise to Yesod's western altar and say:

I give thanks to the power and the presence of Yesod.

Then, using the index finger of your stronger hand, scribe a counterclockwise spiral of violet energy in front of you. Start the spiral at the outer edge and move inward to the center.

Move counterclockwise to Tiphereth's southern altar and say:

I give thanks to the power and the presence of Tiphereth.

Then, using the index finger of your stronger hand, scribe a counterclockwise spiral of yellow energy in front of you. Start the spiral at the outer edge and move inward to the center.

Move counterclockwise to Daath's eastern altar and say:

I give thanks to the power and the presence of Daath.

Then, using the index finger of your stronger hand, scribe a counterclockwise spiral of lavender energy in front of you. Start the spiral at the outer edge and move inward to the center.

Move counterclockwise to Kether's northern altar and say:

I give thanks to the power and the presence of Kether.

Then, using the index finger of your stronger hand, scribe a counterclockwise spiral of white energy in front of you. Start the spiral at the outer edge and move inward to the center.

Lastly, move to the center and say:

This rite is ended. So mote it be.

As a matter of good practice, take time to ground and center, and to return your chakras and energy to their normal levels.

CHAPTER 9

Three Methods for Collective Visioning

The expression "Many hands make light work" is often true when the tasks are physical, but the coordination of the psychic talents of multiple individuals is often hard work in itself. You can certainly pose the same question, the same request, to several practitioners and then compare their views. This method does help find the strongest signal, but it does not blend and combine the talents so much as it averages the results. If the information that is sought is difficult to reach or understand, or the probabilities are widely spread, then a stronger, more refined talent is more useful than a collection of observations. I have developed three methods that make it easier to do collective visioning that can be worked by people at varying levels of skill and talent. Furthermore, doing collective work often has the effect of sparking new growth and development in the participants.

After you read through this chapter, think about those people you know that you would want to invite to try these methods. If you do not have people in your life already that would be appropriate, then this may be an impetus to find some colleagues. If you try these methods, I strongly recommend that all the participants be in the same room. You might see some benefit to using them at a distance working at a synchronized time, perhaps augmented by meeting via the Internet or a similar technology, but metaphysical constraints will impose some limitations. I love technology, and this is not a Luddite rant against its use. I've had an email account since the late 1970s, since the days of the 300-baud modem, and yet I am still the tech maven helping people half my age with their smartphones and tablets.

To truly blend and combine talents, the many layers of auras involved must touch or overlap. A fairly standard model in many esoteric systems describes the human energy field as consisting of layers that go from the densest, being the physical body, up to some varying number of layers that end at the boundary between the individual's energy and that of the universe. These layers are the subtle bodies, and they fit within each other like Russian nesting dolls. It is also part of the standard model of ethereal anatomy that the lower, denser layers are the ones that do most of the heavy lifting in magickal and energetic work. Here's the catch: the denser the subtle body is, the more it resembles the physical form in size and shape, and the less flexible it is. Therefore, the denser subtle bodies cannot stretch very far away from the physical body. Many psychic or magickal actions will work from a great distance, and others will not. There are some workaround solutions to this issue, but they are not easy and are best taught in person.

The Lens

The first method, which I call *the Lens,* uses the division of labor to assist in the work of gathering information. Each participant should apply themselves to only one part of the process so that they can concentrate fully on that portion of the work. The work is divided into four tasks: seeking and collecting; filtering and refining; magnifying and unpacking; and perceiving and understanding. Ideally, each participant should choose to do the role that most closely matches their strengths. Three is the minimum number of participants for this method because one person can take on the tasks of magnifying and perceiving, but four people is better. I am not sure what the maximum number of participants should be. I have had as many as twelve, which did work, but all the contributors to that working were well versed in these matters. The task of perceiving and understanding is usually handled by one person, but it can be handled by up to three people if they can work harmoniously. The Lens can be done very simply and casually, or it can be done as a full-blown ritual.

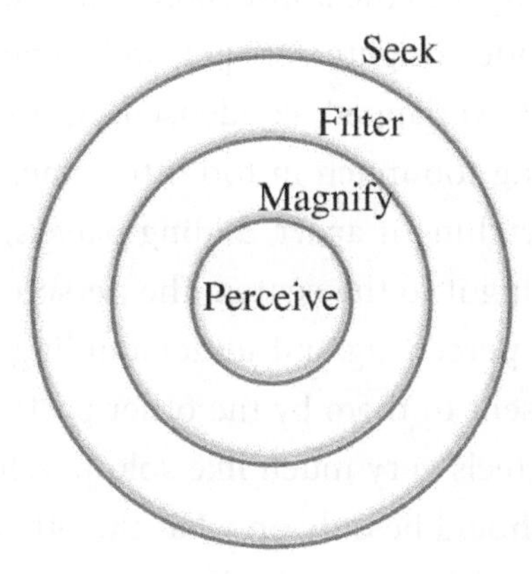

The Four Tasks

Let's say that you have four people and would like to use this method in a quick and straightforward manner. The first step is to determine and assign parts for the working. Arrange four chairs so that one is near the center of the room and the others are arranged outward in a line. You may choose to sit or stand during the working, but having the chairs ready is a good option.

The person who is responsible for seeking and collecting should sit or stand farthest away from the central chair. This person's role in this method is to reach out with their mind, to call out the question, to pull in the energy, to request assistance, and so on. The next person inward is responsible for filtering and refining what has been drawn. Their role in this method is to sort through all the impressions and the information that is being drawn in, and if it feels connected to the question or the intention of the question to push the energy inward. Any impressions that are not related to the matter at hand should be sent downward into the ground. The person just out from the center is responsible for magnifying and unpacking the flow that has been filtered. Their role is to amplify the flow by drawing in energy and adding it to the impressions and the information so that they are louder, brighter, crisper, and so on. Often psychic impressions are overlapped, condensed, or are in high-speed bursts containing too much in too little time. Unpacking the flow means stretching it apart, adding pauses, and slowing it down and sending it to the center. The person in the center is responsible for perceiving and understanding what has been processed and sent to them by the other participants. For the most part, this feels very much like solo psychic work except that the focus should be only on what the others are directing toward the center. The person in the center may vision directly, use skrying tools such as a black mirror, or may use a divinatory system such as the tarot, runes, and so on.

Contingent upon the people and the space you have to work with, you have a few options to consider. If the space is tight, and the people are willing, you may wish to place the chairs close enough to each other so that everyone can hold hands. Holding hands is a sure way to link your energies, but do not link hands to form a circle. If the person who is the central focus is holding hands with the person who is the seeker, this hand-holding short-circuits the process.

When the work is deemed complete, all the participants should share their experiences. It is important that the impressions from the central person be written down; someone else may need to do this for the participants. Then all should proceed with grounding and closing down their subtle senses. It is particularly important to make sure that any linkages that have formed between the participants are closed down and severed as well.

Should you desire to do a more advanced version of the Lens, here are a few options. If you have a big enough room or can do this outside, scribing three concentric circles of energy is an excellent way to enhance this working. This can be done using the power of the mind and a finger, a wand, a crystal, or whatever else suits you. The energy scribing can be done by one person or several, so long as everyone visualizes the circles. The concentric energy circles serve two main purposes: they help to focus the energy inward, and they act as antennas, wave guides, to draw in more information. Marking the boundaries of the circles with tea candles, chalk marks, painters' tape, or something else that is safe and temporary is helpful. At the end of the working, you will need to dissolve the energy of the concentric circles into the ground.

Movement, gesture, and posture can also have an impact on how well you can access your inner senses and manage energy flow. When you include your physical body and your kinesthetic sense in your spiritual work, your Lower Self and its deep awareness of the subtle realms are awakened more fully. Those who are seeking and collecting may wish to face outward from the center with outstretched hands and hailing gestures. Those who are filtering and refining may wish to hold hands or place their hands over the center of their chests. Those who are magnifying and unpacking the flow may wish to point their hands toward the center with sweeping motions. The person or persons in the center hold their hands with palms up, hold hands, or adopt whatever pose maximizes their openness. All the participants can pace, sway, turn slowly in place, or move as they feel called to do so.

The Lens

You may rework this method many different ways to adapt it to your needs, so long as you follow the process that is the mechanism of action of the Lens. You may wish to add poetic language for the investing and claiming of the roles of the participants. Or perhaps you may wish for the person in the center to give a statement of intent before beginning. If those involved are open to toning or chanting, it is a great help in attuning the participants to each other. I encourage you to make this method your own by adding those components that bring you power and clarity.

The Web

Before beginning to explain the method I call *the Web*, I'd like to remind you of the holographic nature of the Lower Self, which I touched on in Chapter 3 on the Three Selves. If you recall, a hologram contains within itself the entire image disseminated throughout every part of the hologram because it is a photograph of the overlapping wave fronts, the interference pattern. This means that if you cut a hologram in half, each half still contains the entire image, though you might have to tilt the hologram to see the whole image. If you cut it into quarters, the same is true. A hologram is like a window of memory, and when divided, each piece is a pane. As the image is divided, it may become grainy due to the nature of the material or require an extreme viewing angle, but it still contains the whole image. Every person is a microcosm of the Universe, and their window pane into the greater whole resides in their Lower Self. This method that I call the Web weaves together the wave fronts, connects the edges of the participants' Lower Selves, so that a larger and clearer image of the whole can be constructed.

This method is best for a group of people who know each other and have trust in each other's skills and intentions. A minimum of four people is needed for this method. I do not recommend more than twenty-five people, and that is pushing the limits. One person should be assigned to be the monitor/facilitator and should not connect their energy to this working. This person should be energy sensitive and fairly experienced, as their role in this method is to watch for safety, and to start and stop the working as they deem appropriate. The facilitator will also help to offer verbal guidance to keep the group on track toward the desired goal of the session. This method can be done without a monitor, though it is less safe that way, and at the very least a timer should be set to end the session.

I am normally a proponent for the value of having highly defined questions or objectives before beginning to do psychic work. The Web is a good method to choose when you are unclear on how to approach a problem or a question because it tends to awaken your instincts and nonverbal wisdom. I encourage you to define your goals as much as you can before you start the work, but the facilitator can help continue to refine the goals and questions during the session. Make sure that there is ample time for queries and discussions so that everyone is clear on the question(s) before the working.

The process for the Web is as follows:

1. Reduce the lighting in the room and make sure that the temperature is comfortable for everyone. It is a good idea to have a few blankets and throw pillows handy as well. The group should sit or lie down and find comfortable positions that they can stay in throughout the session. Once all are in their positions, the facilitator should help guide the group through grounding, centering, and a gentle opening of the inner senses, such as intoning IAO.

2. All the participants should rub their hands together and draw some energy up into their hands. All the participants except the facilitator should then place themselves in physical contact with the people nearest to them. This connection can be touching fingers, holding hands, touching a shoulder, linking arms, draping legs over each other, and so on. Only the lightest physical touch is needed, and it can be through clothing. The goal is to have a web of physical contact that connects everyone except the facilitator. Some people may need to relocate, depending on needs related to physical or emotional comfort. The particular shape of the grouping is not important. The facilitator is responsible for making this part of the process as smooth as possible.

3. Then the group does a few cycles of counted Four-Fold Breathing. After a few cycles, the participants should return to normal breathing and close their eyes. Next, the facilitator should guide the group in imagining their

auras expanding and expanding, breath by breath, until they feel their aura overlap the auras of the people nearest to them. The participants should be encouraged to hear and feel the rhythm, the beat, of their united energy.

4. The facilitator then reminds the participants of the intended goal of the session. The participants are encouraged to quietly speak aloud any key elements of what they are perceiving during the session. Then the visioning begins, with the facilitator keeping a close eye on the individuals and the overall feel of the group. As the session progresses, the facilitator may guide the flow by occasionally adding a word, a phrase, or a reframing of the question as needed. This step is especially important if the session is exploratory or centered on an open-ended question.

5. When it seems that no new information is being gleaned or the group is beginning to tire, it is time to end the session. The facilitator guides the group through two short stints of rapid, shallow breathing alternated with breath holding. The participants are told to imagine their auras disengaging from each other and becoming tight and close to their bodies. They all break physical contact from each other. They all say their name out loud at least three times. The group is guided through grounding and centering again. The participants are encouraged to tap their hands together, to touch their faces, stand up, or move in whatever way they like.

6. The facilitator should then make sure all the participants are fully present and that their energy is returning to normal. After that, it is time for sharing, summarizing, and synthesizing the material that was received. It is a good

idea to have some food and drink as people are sharing their impressions because that helps prevent them from sliding back into an energetically connected state. Some people are drawn to eating sweets after this type of work, which is fine, but they should be encouraged to eat something with a higher protein content to help the grounding process.

Keeping a log or journal of these sessions is the best way to ensure that the information gathered in the Web can be understood and put to use. It is also important to be aware that participants in the Web may remain partly tuned in to each other for some time after the session is over, even if it was closed down properly. This may result in flashes of intuition about each other's circumstances and states of being. Whether or not this is a good thing will depend on many variables.

Seething or Stirring the Cauldron

The method I call *the Cauldron* requires a minimum of two participants and a maximum of six, and is a better match for people who can let go and be spontaneous. This method can be done standing, but it works better with the participants seated in a circle in chairs or seated on the floor with pillows or mats. This method differs from the others in this chapter in that it does not blend the psychic perceptions of the participants; instead, the group interaction enlivens and impels the individual talents. The group's efforts create a viewing portal that exceeds what would be done by them as individuals.

When people are in a race together, they can often achieve faster times as they push to match or exceed the pace of the others. When a group of people are singing together, they are more inclined to sing louder and to take chances with hitting notes at the edges of their ranges. A similar principle applies to collective visioning work. Another distinction in this method is that participants may be focused on different questions or pursuits during the same session.

While it is always a good idea to turn off phones, close doors, and make sure that animals and loved ones won't disturb your session, it is vital that you assure this for the Cauldron. Emotions and energies can be quite high during the use of this method, and interruptions can be very jarring. Make sure that you have had some water and a bathroom break before beginning. During the performance of the Cauldron, you will be rocking back and forth or swaying. Initially, you will be holding hands, but that may change as the session proceeds, so position yourselves accordingly. I prefer using this method seated on the floor in a tight circle, but the needs and comfort of the group are the determining factor. Dimmed lighting is better, and barring allergies and sensitivities, incense will also help set a proper atmosphere for the working.

To begin, sit and hold hands to form a circle. Breathe together for a minute or two and then begin to tone softly. You may intone any vowel sound or AUM, and all the participants may choose a different sound if they like. It is important to listen to the sounds that the others are making and strive to make sounds that are harmonious with the whole. Begin to sway or move gently as a group. As you move, imagine that you are rocking your power back and forth. Become aware of the feel of the energy pulsing around the circle. The space in the center of the circle is the cauldron. After a while, begin a pattern of pushing and pulling your hands toward the center of the circle. With each push inward, see a sphere of light forming in the center of the circle. You may gaze into the ball of light with your eyes open or close your eyes and direct your inner gaze to the center. You may listen or open any and all of your psychic senses.

Allow the sounds and the movements of the group to emerge, change, and evolve over the course of the session. There will probably be periods of silence as well as more toning. Avoid conversations and full sentences, but speak a word or two if you need to during the Cauldron. The session will have one or more peaks of intensity, and, at some point, one or more of the participants will reach their limit and the working should end. If you are tired and need to conclude the session, stop whatever rocking or swaying that you are doing. Gradually, try to stop the motion of your hands if you are still holding hands with someone. Hopefully, others will take the clue and do the same. If that is not the case, gently release their hands, and say "To Earth, to Earth, to Earth!" with each repetition louder than the last.

All the participants should reposition themselves so that they are no longer facing each other in a circle. Then use any and all of the techniques that you have at your disposal to ground, center, and close down your subtle senses. After taking some time to write down and/or share your impressions, be sure to have some food and drink. At the very least, place a few grains of salt on your tongue because that will do much to return you to a normal state of being. If you are feeling clear-headed but overly charged up, go to a sink and let the water run over your wrists. The running water helps carry away the excess energy.

CHAPTER 10

Working with Minerals

Countless sources of information are available on the metaphysical uses and virtues of gems, minerals, and stones. More than five thousand different types of minerals have been discovered, and more are yet to be uncovered. There has been an explosion in the accessibility of crystal shops, mineral shows, and online storefronts. This abundance of options can be overwhelming to people who are newly interested in working with minerals.

This chapter focuses on gems, minerals, and stones that are of use in clarifying and improving psychic perception and that are of moderate cost and easy to find. In addition to giving information about their inherent qualities, this chapter also includes techniques and tips to make them work with your psychism. For those of you who may be considering skipping or skimming through this chapter, because you have not felt a connection to working with crystals in the past, please give the material a close reading. I have had students who were sure that they had no use for crystals discover that they had new additions to their bag of tricks after a few lessons.

The Mineral Kingdom

Have you heard the question "Is it animal, vegetable, or mineral?" as a part of a game like Twenty Questions? A fuller and older form of the question asks if something is a part of the animal, plant, or mineral kingdom. Animal, vegetable, and mineral also denote the three branches of Alchemical practice. No doubt, you've heard of the concept of dividing life into plant life or animal life. Often in the Twenty Questions game, mineral is the category for nonliving objects, but that is a matter of perspective. If life is defined only by processes that are observed in animals and plants, then minerals are not alive. However, by such a strict definition, then, viruses would not be considered living things. The more closely we look, the less clear the boundary between what is living and what is not becomes, even if we limit ourselves to the perspectives of science.

In addition, our knowledge of life is limited to one incompletely studied planet in a very large cosmos. If you are reading this book, it is safe to say that you have concluded that there are forces beyond what has as of yet been measured by the physical sciences. My understanding of the universe is that every manifested part of it is imbued with spirit; this means that gems, minerals, and stones partake of the spirit of the universe. They may not have carbon-based organic life, but to my eyes, everything physical has spirit and therefore life of a sort.

To begin, let's define some terms:

- A *mineral* is a specific combination of elements forming a naturally occurring compound that often, but not necessarily, takes on a crystalline form, depending on the conditions of its formation.

- A *stone*, or rock, is a collection of multiple materials and may be inorganic or a combination of organic and inorganic materials.
- *Gems* are stones, minerals, or organic materials, such as pearls, that are cut, adapted, shaped, or polished for use in jewelry and decorative objects.
- A *crystal* is a solid whose atoms (or molecules and ions) are organized in an orderly and repeating pattern that extends throughout its entirety.

The shape of a crystal is in part determined by its lattice, its template, and in part by the conditions under which it formed. Crystals grow and seek equilibrium with their environment, and many can react to stimuli. Some crystals can reproduce after a fashion, in that under the right conditions a piece that is broken off can act as the nucleus for another crystal to grow. When the conditions are right, a crystal broken in its environment of origin will begin to heal the broken area and reestablish order. It is remarkable how many ways crystals come close to the definitions applied to biological life. For the sake of simplicity, I'll use the word *crystal* as a catchall term in most cases in this chapter.

Crystals can take seconds, years, centuries, or thousands of years to form, depending on the variety of crystal and the conditions of their origin. Most of the crystals that you are likely to work with took many years to form and are tens of thousands to millions of years old. As an example, a large quartz point of the size you would place on a staff took about a thousand years to form and a million or so years to find its way close enough to the surface of the Earth so that it could be collected.

Why does knowing these details matter? It helps encourage reverence and wonder for the crystals that we use in our work. It may be that they are now relatively inexpensive and easy to obtain, but they are older than any antique or heirloom. Your attitude helps shape the way your energy interacts with crystals.

There is also a metaphysical reason that the age of crystals is significant. The longer something has existed in the physical plane, the stronger and more palpable a presence it has in the other planes of being. One well-accepted principle is that time behaves differently on each plane of being. Time is experienced as being more linear and discrete with high causality on the physical plane and becomes more nonlinear and nonlocal with high synchronicity on each plane above the physical. Crystals, as a result of the length of their physical existence, can act as a useful anchor and platform for working with multiple planes of being in a synchronized fashion. In other words, they make it easier to act in and to navigate the realms beyond the physical, which is useful in matters of psychic perception. You exist in multiple planes of being at once; each layer of your aura is resident to its corresponding higher plane. The substantial energetic presence that crystals have on multiple planes of being make it easier to become aware of the parts of you that exist in those other levels of reality.

When artists are asked to depict crystals, by and large they draw minerals with clearly defined facets and clean geometries. These are called euhedral crystals, and their microscopic structure is clearly visible in the macroscopic appearance. Quartz is a common euhedral crystal. The more ideal the growth environment for the crystal, the more well formed its geometry. In addition to the beauty that you see in the shapes of crystals, there is also an expression of several metaphysical principles. In euhedral crystals, you can see an exemplar of the Hermetic

Axiom of "as above, so below" in the strong linkage between the smallest structure (atomic crystal lattice) and the expansion of that same structure to the scale of an object that can be held.

Crystals can also be said to display the *doctrine of signatures* in their forms. In traditional herbalism, the outward appearance of plants in their form, color, scent, texture, and other features shows the signature of their inner spiritual nature and properties. The appearance of crystals, whether or not they are euhedral, also offers clues to their energetic properties and uses to those that can read their signatures. The suggestion of a similarity of natures between herbs and crystals is useful. They both have properties that can assist in spiritual endeavors when they are used properly. The plant and mineral kingdoms, though they have spirit, do not exhibit consciousness in the mode that animals do.

Crystals do not have waking consciousness and personalities in the sense that humans do, but they do have characters, tendencies, and intrinsic natures. I know practitioners who communicate with their crystals, and they report experiencing this as a two-way dialogue. If it suits your temperament, this may be a practical approach, but it is my belief that this is an artifact of human consciousness interacting with the energetic templates of crystals. If you experience words and images in your communion with crystals, they are drawn from your mind. Crystals have spiritual beingness, but not representational awareness. As a comparison to something similar, though not the same, plants can act with purpose and intelligence without the recourse of words, images, or a centralized nervous system.

Furthermore, one of the devices that humans use to make sense of things is to anthropomorphize or vivimorphize, to attribute human or animal traits, to objects, forces, processes, and entities, thus creating a practical interface regardless of whether or not it is strictly true. I will also remind you that crystals exist in multiple planes and have a palpable aura in the other realms, which means that they can also act as conduits of connection to nonphysical beings. If a crystal truly appears to be exhibiting interactive consciousness, then it may be good to ask if something is speaking through the crystal rather than the crystal itself.

Getting Started with Crystals for Psychic Work

Crystals took a long time to come into being and find their way into your hands, so you may wish to take it slow as well. It is easy to quickly amass a collection of crystals that may be lovely to behold but that you do not know well or use well. I recommend that you start with no more than five or six different types of crystals. If you already have dozens of crystals in pouches, jewelry, on altars, on your nightstand, and pretty much everywhere in your home, pick five or six different types of crystals and ignore the rest for a time.

If you spend enough time learning the qualities, uses, and the feel of a small set of crystals, you will learn the knack for developing a connection with all types of crystals. Think of the crystals as each being like a musical instrument. Once a musician has learned one or two instruments well, it is easier to pick up other instruments. If that comparison doesn't work for you, think of them like cars, sewing machines, or if you prefer a biological example, horses. Each type will be different, but what you learn with one type accelerates learning in the next one.

Procedures and Protocols for Using Crystals

Most crystals will give you some benefit related to their list of uses and attributes, simply by having them touch your skin or their being close enough to you to interact with your aura. However, this is less than optimal, so the assistance the crystals provide will be low level and generic. A bit of magick, or energy work if you prefer to call it that, brings out more in a crystal. It is like the difference between a massage practitioner who is competent in the physical practice and the amazing results that come from one who knows how to move energy while giving a massage. It is also like the difference between an incense that is a mixture of all the right herbs and resins for a given purpose and one that has had the spirits of the plants awakened before burning.

Priming the crystals and setting them for specific purposes tuned to your energy yield significant results. There are many methods for preparing crystals and rationales for each approach. For the sake of brevity, as this is not a book focused on crystals, I share a few of my favorite methods. I recommend you learn how to use these methods using a clear quartz, ideally a natural point, as the material for your first efforts. Quartz is easy to obtain, it is inexpensive, and it has perhaps the greatest range of uses and is very adaptable. By the way, don't worry about finding perfectly transparent quartz; for these purposes, inclusions, clouds, and so on are fine. Clear quartz is almost a blank slate that readily takes the mark of intentions and instructions. As such, it will be more responsive to your input, and this will give you clearer feedback on whether or not you are achieving your aims. The process I use for working with crystals uses five steps: cleansing, preparing, programming, empowering, and using.

Cleansing

By the time a crystal comes into your possession, it has passed through many hands and absorbed a variety of energies and patterns. Even if you dug the crystal out of the ground with your own hands, you have no way of knowing what has occurred at that site. It is prudent to cleanse crystals not only when you first acquire them but also periodically because they can pick up unwanted influences. Unless you feel the crystal is strongly imbued with unwanted things, a simple cleansing will suffice. There are many methods for cleansing crystals, but I will share just a few; experiment with different methods until you find the ones that suit your needs and style.

The most direct and uncomplicated mode of purification is to hold a crystal under running water while pushing brilliant white energy through the crystal until it feels clean. More often than not, this is enough in the same way that soap and water will suffice and an autoclave is overkill.

Some crystals are quickly damaged by water, such as desert rose, halite, and other mineral salts, so cleansing with water is not safe for them. Some crystals, such as selenite, malachite, and opal, can be exposed to water briefly, if they are dried quickly after cleansing them, but they will be damaged by lengthy immersion. Check on the nature of a crystal before rinsing or soaking it, especially if you've added salt to the water, as is so often suggested. Another easy option is to pass the crystal through incense, such as frankincense, sage, copal, palo santo, or your preferred purification herb or resin, while pushing a stream of brilliant white energy through it.

If you need a more thorough cleansing, place the crystal on a plate; silver or silver-plated is best, though ceramic will do. Find three tea candles, votives in glass, or some other candle that can burn safely on a table or altar. Take each candle, one at a time, and hold it to your chest, while envisioning a flame that is pure and resplendent with the light of the Sun, the Moon, and the Stars.

Take a breath and blow into each candle the intention that the candle's light will be the light of purity. Place the three candles around the plate, forming a triangle, and light them. Look upon the flames and see the unwanted energies rising from the crystals and being consumed by the flames. Spend as much time as you like watching over the cleansing. If it is safe to do so, you may leave the candles burning and return to snuff them out at least an hour later. Afterward, place the crystal outdoors so that it is in the Sun for an hour or two, followed by an hour or two under the Moon and Stars.

I make a distinction between cleansing a crystal and *clearing* a crystal. You may have a crystal that you have been using for some time that is not contaminated with extraneous patterns or energies, but that you want to put to a purpose very different from what you've done with it in the past. In this case, it needs to be cleared of the programming and the habits of use that are ingrained within it. Sometimes the cleansing methods will not fully remove these deeply set patterns unless you repeat them several times. I have found that sound is very effective at stripping out these patterns. For example, you can hold a crystal with your hand and bring it near to your mouth. While pushing energy through the crystal with your hand, intone AUM or a vowel sound. See the sound vibrating the crystal and dislodging and breaking up the patterns that are then swept away by the current of energy. It really is best if you use your voice, but if for whatever reason you cannot, another option is to use a bell or singing bowl. It is also important that you focus your attention on clearing away any instructions or routines that are within the crystal. It is your consciousness interacting with the crystal that is really doing the work.

You may have encountered the teaching that some crystals do not need cleansing or clearing because they are naturally resistant to becoming contaminated. Some authors and teachers go so far as to say that it is impossible for certain crystals to become tainted. I agree that some crystals are resistant, but under the right circumstances, *all* crystals can become coated or imbued with inappropriate or unpleasant energy. I have seen crystals that are supposed to be inherently benign charged with the power to cause illness and harm. Use your own judgment and your own psychic senses, but I would rather err on the side of safety, so I cleanse all my crystals.

Preparing

In the next step, the preparatory work is as much about preparing you as it is preparing the crystal. Before you can engage with the crystal, you need to attune yourself to the crystal. You are more adaptable than the crystal. To work with the crystal, you need to adjust yourself to find the channel, or frequency, metaphorically speaking, where it operates. I describe two techniques that can be used singly or in unison to attune yourself to a crystal.

Finding Its Heartbeat

You may be seated or standing for this technique. Place the crystal in front of you on a table or counter, ideally so that the crystal is at the same height as your heart. Close your eyes, breathe slowly, and move into the state of mind that you use for meditation, psychic work, or magick. Become aware of the flows of life within you: breath, blood, and subtle energies. Envision the glow of your subtle bodies, your aura, around you. Slowly, breath by breath, expand your aura outward until you can feel the lightest touch pressing back; that is the energy of the crystal. Do not push your energy any further; simply pay attention to the fluctuations in the energy of the crystal. Think of this as feeling for the pulse of the crystal. Imagine it as listening for the rhythm of the beat that is energy moving in and through the crystal. Become familiar with the feel of the crystal's heartbeat because it will become a key to working with the crystal.

Finding Its Voice

As with the previous technique, you may be seated or standing for this technique. Hold the crystal with both hands. Steady and prepare yourself in whatever may be your normal fashion, and draw energy into yourself either up from the ground or down from the heavens, whichever is easier. Then take a breath and make a tone with your voice; this can be an AUM or any vowel sound. While toning, push energy into the crystal, and pay attention to the ease or resistance offered by the crystal as you do so. Pause, take a breath, and repeat the process with a higher or a lower note. Continue experimenting until you find the note or notes that represent the place where your energy and that of the crystal are most compatible. Having established the proper range for the energy, alternate between pushing energy through the crystal and drawing energy into you via the crystal while toning. When you feel that the crystal is awakened and energized, stop moving energy with your will and listen for the resonance that is the crystal's voice.

If neither of these methods suits you, or you have a tried-and-true method that you prefer for connecting yourself to a crystal, please use it before undertaking the next step in the preparations. It has been my experience that most crystals are at this point ready for receiving programming, embedded instructions, but all benefit from one more action before proceeding. Any crystal that you hold has been separated from its place of origin and often has been broken to some degree. As such, the crystal's aura may have weaknesses that range from minimal to significant but could be improved with energetic healing or reshaping. Since the structure of crystals is so deeply ordered, in most situations the overall energy characteristics are intact and/or have achieved a new equilibrium with their environment, so only a little repair is needed. This is especially true of crystals composed of many small interlocking crystals. In the case of crystals with clearly defined faces, damage is more readily evident and remains present even if it has been cut or polished away. Crystals that have been reshaped into spheres, pyramids, and other shapes exhibit an aura that is a combination of their inherent structure and the geometry of their outer form.

Healing or repairing the energy is optional fine-tuning, but often worth the additional effort. To do this, connect with the energy of the crystal and examine it closely. Use whichever combination of psychic sensory modalities you have, such as feeling, hearing, and seeing, to find the places in the aura of the crystal that you experience as weak, inharmonious, or out of balance. Then tune in to the specific energy pattern of the crystal that you discovered earlier, and pour energy into the places that need reinforcement. If you are a healer, you can adapt the methods you use on people. Use your aura and your power of imagination to smooth and remold the aura of the crystal until it feels in harmony.

Programming

In the programming part of the process, the objective is to anchor your desired behaviors and outcomes to the crystal's inherent nature. A secondary but important objective is to ensure that the programming is durable and will last for some time. The word *programming* in this context is a computing metaphor that suggests that we are inserting lines of code, or instructions, into the crystal or perhaps downloading a useful app into the crystal. This use of the concept of programming a crystal is ubiquitous in the community of crystal practitioners. Crystals were put to use for spiritual and magickal practices long before Ada Lovelace, the mother and prophet of computing, first described a program in the mid-1850s. An older way of instilling purpose into crystals is the process of consecration. Much of what is done in the consecration of tools used in rituals also applies to crystals. Here, I offer suggestions on how to program a crystal, how to consecrate a crystal, and a blending of the two approaches.

To begin programming a crystal, first take some time to ground and center yourself. Then close your eyes and move inward to your inner landscape. See yourself standing in your center, shining with your light. Reinforce the feeling of being in your inner sanctum; then gently open your eyes and pick up the crystal. Close your eyes again and walk toward the crystal held in your hands. Depending on your sensibilities, the crystal may appear as a cave, a building, a stone circle, or any number of things, but you will recognize it. Whichever way that you see it, the crystal will be large enough for you to step into it. Explore and become familiar with the inside of the crystal.

Consider the purpose that you intend for the crystal because that will determine what comes next. For instance, let's say that you intend to use the crystal as an aid to your psychic sight. I might envision the crystal as filled with microscopes, with telescopes, and with viewing screens filling the walls. Depending on your preferences, you may see the crystal as having a well filled with swirling mists and waters that show images, with skrying mirrors on every surface, and perhaps an all-seeing eye floating above the crystal. The aim is to fill the crystal with whatever objects and symbols speak to you and reinforce the intended purpose for the crystal. This method is somewhat like the process of setting up a *memory palace*. You need not limit yourself to inanimate objects. You can populate the interior of the crystal with people or animals if you imagine them as helpers.

If you have programmed crystals before using more customary methods, you may have noted that we haven't used words as the primary tool for programming. The process of filling the crystal with physical representations of the intended work touches deeper layers of your psyche. The process also creates thought forms that become anchored to the crystal's energetic pattern. In my method, the last step in programming a crystal is the pronouncing of intentions and affirmations that act as a linkage to your waking consciousness. You can achieve decent results with just the use of words, but I have found that there are better results and a deeper and more lasting imprint upon a crystal when those words are written on constructs that you have embedded within the crystal. Often the process of filling the crystal with appropriate images and constructs will refine which words that you use as the final mark to seal the programming.

Consecration of a crystal can be used in lieu of programming or as an adjunct to programming. When something is consecrated, a connection is made between it and the sacred. Consecration is the sanctification of either a person, a place, or an object. It can also be the process of dedicating someone or something to a specific spiritual purpose. When you consecrate a crystal, you are connecting it to your belief structure and/or one or more of the spiritual entities that you work with. In other words, you are asking for the help, protection, and support of a God/dess, ancestor, angel, and so on in the work that you intend to do with the crystal. Your conviction and commitment to a specific form of religion or spirituality to a great degree determine the effectiveness of the consecration. The style and format for the consecration of a crystal are set by your practices and whatever the traditional ritual patterns may be for the being in question. Additionally, a crystal that has been consecrated needs to be treated with the respect that is due to a sanctified object.

You should treat all crystals that you have prepared to use in your work with respect, but if you have connected them to a spiritual force, to an entity, that care and respect become more important.

Empowering

Often, this next step, empowering, is referred to as the charging of the crystal, as if it were a battery or a reservoir for energy of a particular sort. This is a valid and useful way to work with crystals and, in many situations, is a most efficient paradigm. I prefer to call it *empowering* a crystal as a broader category that contains, but is not limited to, the model of a battery. Crystals vary in their capacity to take a charge, the length of time the charge or empowerment will hold, their rate of flow of energy, and their ease or difficulty in taking or releasing energy. As you work more with crystals, you'll find which methods of empowerment work best with the ones you have. Let's start with charging methods and then cover some techniques to empower crystals.

The most direct approach to charging a crystal is to put it in a circuit of power flowing through your body. Hold the crystal with both of your hands, or press it between your palms, while directing energy from your dominant hand through the crystal and into your receptive hand. Raise energy by breathing, toning, visualizing, or whatever method suits you. Keep the energy flowing in a loop that includes the crystal, and feel it fill with more and more energy with each cycle. You will know when the crystal is reaching the limit of its capacity when it becomes harder to push energy through the crystal. This method of charging has the tendency to make it easier to activate and use the crystal, but the charge tends not to be as long lasting.

If your goal is to maximize the length of time that the crystal will hold the charge, then begin by holding the crystal in only your dominant hand. Proceed with raising energy using whichever methods work best for you. Continue to raise energy until you feel that you are holding as much energy as you can; then release your full store of energy into the crystal. Think of this action as grounding the energy into the crystal. Repeat the pattern of raising your energy to a peak and releasing it into the crystal. After several cycles, the crystal will stop taking additional energy. You will know this because you will feel the need to ground to the Earth or send the excess energy skyward to avoid discomfort. Crystals that are charged in this manner will hold that charge for a long period of time whether they are in use or in storage. The cost of this stability is that it takes more effort to activate the crystals, and they also tend to operate at a lower power level.

Many practitioners also recommend placing a crystal outdoors under the light of the Sun or Moon as a method of charging the crystal. For specialized purposes, there is sometimes the suggestion of placing the crystal outside on a windy day, during a storm, and so on. From my perspective, these techniques allow a crystal to reestablish the normal level of energy that is its equilibrium with the environment. This may be enough, depending on the intended uses for the crystal, but this technique does not add energy beyond the basic default state of the crystal. This is often enough for the most common uses for crystals, but it is somewhat less effective if you are trying to use them as an aid to your psychic abilities.

Empowering a crystal, from my perspective, also means giving the crystal a way to collect, funnel, and concentrate energy into itself from the environment. This means modifying the outward form of the crystal's aura so that it will continue to gain energy beyond its inherent set point. In addition to the power invested into the crystal by the practitioner, the crystal will also gain power from the environment even when it is not actively engaged with the practitioner. Empowering a crystal is somewhat like programming a crystal, except that the exterior aura of the crystal is modified with thought forms. In truth, this is a form of spell work.

For example, I have a crystal that I use for extending the range of sending forth my energetic voice. After I charged that crystal, I pulled strands of energy out from within the crystal and shaped them into a helix on a spindle that extends beyond the physical edges of the crystal. We are always surrounded by moving currents of energy. Some of these currents are caused by the wake of the auras of living beings in motion, some are caused by celestial tides, some are moved by Earth energies. The helix and spindle that I attached to my communication crystal catch those currents like a sail or a windmill and draw power down into itself.

I have another crystal that I use for psychic sight, especially in confused or murky situations. I regularly charge it under the Sun and the Moon. The mode of this crystal's empowerment is that I have placed a series of energetic mirrors and lenses over the crystal so that it can draw more light into its core. If you can build a construct in your mind that gathers and focuses power from the environment, you have the first part of empowering a crystal. The second part is anchoring it in the crystal's aura, which you can do if you have attuned yourself to the crystal. Feel free to experiment and let your imagination be your guide in creating empowered crystals.

Using

After preparing a crystal for use, many people will simply pick up the crystal or put it on if it has been mounted as a form of jewelry and assume that it will simply do its job. The assumption is that the crystal will assist in whatever the task at hand may be, and that is generally enough for most of the common uses people have for crystals. Psychic perception, on the other hand, requires greater coordination and finesse, so I recommend establishing a protocol that you use to activate your crystals for these purposes. Let's say that you have a crystal that you have prepared to improve your psychic hearing. You may wish to touch that crystal to the places behind your ears that are the anchoring points for psychic hearing and reach out your energy so that it connects with the crystal. Consider the manner in which you programmed the crystal, and bring that up in your mind so that it becomes active in both yourself and the crystal. Breathe and take a moment to make sure that your flow and rhythm of energy are in sync with those of the crystal. Then begin whatever work you mean to accomplish, periodically checking in to make sure you are still connected to and in sync with the crystal. When you have gained confidence with the use of crystals, you need not be in direct physical contact with the crystal. As long as it is close enough so that you can reach out your energy and form a strong connection, it is close enough.

It is also prudent to develop a customary manner to deactivate, to disengage, from the crystal. Merely putting away the crystal does not necessarily close the connection. It may continue at a reduced level for some time. Remaining connected to the crystal when the work is done makes it difficult to truly shut down your psychic senses, which can lead to harm. To disengage from the crystal, focus on bringing whatever process is ongoing within your programming of the crystal to a stop. Pull back whatever parts of your aura and energy you extended to connect with the crystal. It might be useful to see the light around the crystal dimming to indicate that it is gone dormant, or perhaps to hear the sound of an engine winding down and stopping to give you and the crystal a symbolic message that the work is done. You can deactivate your connection to the crystal in any number of ways. So long as you feel that your psychic senses are no longer being affected by the crystal, then that is enough.

A Short List of Suggested Crystals

I have a pouch, my crane bag, filled with crystals that I carry with me when I am doing psychic or ritual work away from my home. Over the years, I've learned that the eighteen crystals whose qualities and uses I describe here end up being packed in my bag of tricks the most frequently. This is a short list of crystals that are helpful in opening and refining the psychic senses. As you do your research, you'll find many additional uses and applications for the crystals that I've listed.

Here, I focus on the characteristics that are most useful for psychic work, as well as those that are useful in managing and mending the injuries and strains that may derive from psychic work. This list is intentionally short so that you can build confidence and competency. The order of the list is alphabetical, not in order of importance. If you do some reading and research, you'll find many more, and you may add or substitute crystals on this list with others as you gain more experience.

Amethyst

Often called the stone of sobriety, amethyst is useful in helping settle the turbulent emotions that lead to the abuse of substances. It is also used in managing the condition of being intoxicated with overwrought emotions. It is fairly common to be in a situation in which you must use your psychic senses, and you are strongly emotionally engaged with the outcome of what you might discover.

This crystal is one of your best allies when you need to use your psychic senses and your meditative techniques have not been enough to bring you serenity. It is thought to transmute lower energies to higher energies, to shift the frequencies from lower ones to higher ones; this may be one of the reasons that it has a strong calming influence. This property of elevating energy also makes amethyst useful if you are trying to communicate with beings operating above or outside the normal range of your consciousness. It is also useful in shifting your focus of consciousness to higher planes of being.

Apophyllite

The mineral apophyllite comes in a variety of shapes and colors, but I recommend the clear form that grows in pyramidal crystals. It is one of the best crystals for opening the Third Eye and improving psychic seeing, in general. Hold the flat base of this crystal on your brow, where the Third Eye is located, and let the energy from the crystal move back and connect with the pineal gland. Making this a regular exercise helps improve your psychic sight. This crystal is also valuable in efforts to engage in astral travel or other forms of spiritual journeying. If you or someone you are working with has received a psychic shock or trauma, this crystal can be used in reseating displaced auric layers.

Calligraphy Stone

Calligraphy Stone, also known as Miriam Stone, Maryam, and Elephant Skin Jasper, is not a mineral but is a combination of different materials. These stones often come from the mountains in India and are composed of hematite, iron, and, most importantly, shell fossils. This combination of minerals and organically derived material gives this stone the capacity to serve as a bridge between different kingdoms of being and forms of consciousness.

When you are engaged in psychic or spiritual work, it is fairly common to receive vivid impressions but have difficulty in expressing what has been received and words that others can understand. Calligraphy Stone helps bridge this gap between that which has been received and that which can be spoken. It increases the lucidity and eloquence of both the spoken and written communications of your spiritual experiences.

For some, Calligraphy Stone may also encourage or awaken capacities such as automatic writing. Please note that the term *Calligraphy Stone* (*Shu Fa Stone*) is also used to describe a type of botryoidal fluorite that is not the same as the purposes described here. Shu Fa Stone does assist in stimulating the Third Eye and Crown Chakras and gives more color and clarity to inner sight.

Enhydro Quartz

Enhydro quartz is a type of quartz that has tiny drops of water encapsulated within the inside of the crystal during its formation. Sometimes there are gases, sand, or oil mixed in so that you can see a moving bubble within the small chambers. More often than not, the drop or drops cannot be seen to move. Some enhydro crystals are mostly clear, but more commonly they have a variety of inclusions. All these variations work well for psychic work. These crystals can be used to encourage or to control empathy. They are also useful for journeys to the underworld, the deep subconscious, and all hidden places. They can also be used to enter into the trances, dreams, or coma states of other people to help them find their way out. This is risky work, and I hesitate to share this information, so I ask that you use it responsibly.

Fluorite

The mineral fluorite comes in a wide range of colors and also can take on many different crystalline shapes. For most of the purposes described in this book, a tumbled fluorite of any color will do. If they are available, octahedral fluorites are the best option, and those that are blue or purple are more effective. Fluorite transmutes higher energies to lower energies, which is why it is often perceived to be a stone useful in grounding. In truth, it is not assisting in grounding, but it is shifting energies closer to the range of what is comfortable for the practitioner. It is particularly useful if a person has been spending too much time in an altered state of consciousness; is engaged in mediumship, skrying, or some other work that uses the psychic skills intensively; and needs help finding their way back into normal consciousness. When used in combination with amethyst, fluorite can also be used to recharge the depleted aura.

Larvikite

Larvikite is a stone composed of a mixture of minerals and is also known as Black Labradorite, Norwegian Moonstone, Crone Stone, and Blue Pearl Granite. Feldspar is the primary mineral in larvikite. It stimulates and augments inner psychic vision and remote viewing; plus, it increases the range backward or forward in time for your perceptions. Larvikite also helps improve both connecting with and understanding nature spirits and the fae. When you have a vague, unformed impression that you just can't quite grasp, larvikite helps bring it to the surface so that you can examine it more closely. This stone can also be used to reawaken psychic talents that have gone dormant and to heal talents damaged by overuse.

Molybdenite (Pure or in Quartz)

Molybdenite is the mineral form of the metal molybdenum. The pure crystals are somewhat fragile, so it is more practical to use quartz crystals with molybdenite, though they are harder to find. Its greatest value is that it melds or fuses together tears and cuts in layers of the aura or in fields of energy. As such, it can be used to heal wounds of a nonphysical nature. But please be sure that the wounds are clean, lest you seal something in that you do not want. You can also use this stone to join together energies or patterns that normally would fly apart. An example of this is in creating spell constructs or in connecting the programming between several crystals. Molybdenite can also be used to bind together two or three practitioners' energies so that they can share and combine their talents. This is a risky operation and sometimes requires a forceful severing of the connection when the work is done.

Nuummite

Nuummite is an unusual rock from Greenland that is doubly metamorphic, and it is one of the oldest stones on the planet. Small amounts of it have also been found in Spain, Canada, and the United States. Nuummite is about three billion years old. Following the principle that the longer something has been itself on the physical plane, the more tangible and powerful it is on the subtle planes, this is the ideal stone for the psychic, the witch, or the magician. It strengthens the auric field, draws on the elemental forces, and deflects negative energies. It can also be used as a focal point for your power and is a great stone when facing fears. In addition, it has a great capacity for the storage of information and patterns, such as preset spells and procedures. For many, it also tends to sharpen their psychic perceptions. It is also good as a component in objects such as pendulums, runes, spirit boards, or other divinatory tools. Try to find a pendant, ring, small tumbled stone, a wand, or any other form that you can keep close to your skin.

Obsidian (Black)

Obsidian is really volcanic glass and comes in a variety of colors. All of them are valuable, but begin with black obsidian. It is the stone of truth. If you are questioning your perspective or your perception of a situation, then hold this stone and push some of your energy into it and draw it back out into yourself. Repeat this process while reviewing your perspective and your perception.

Black obsidian is also a powerful stone for skrying, either as a black mirror or on a ring or pendant as a cabochon. As a blade, it can be used to draw out and ground negative energies or magical energetic poisons. The value of an obsidian mirror as a tool for skrying is that it provides a certain amount of defense against being observed by that which you are observing. You can also use an obsidian mirror to see hidden energies or beings. Rather than using it for skrying, use it to catch the reflection of subtle energies. Get the shape of obsidian that suits the way that you intend to use it first. It is fragile, so package it well because it chips and scratches easily. Eventually, you'll want several different shapes of obsidian.

Pearl and Coral

Although pearl and coral are not technically stones or minerals, for our purposes, they've been included in this category. While pearl is better at affecting more layers of the aura at once, coral functions almost as well and is cheaper and more abundant. Unlike the other crystals and stones in this suggested set where the intended magickal usage is an inherent property of the material, pearl and coral require your focused energetic intention to act in the way that is needed. Unlike stibnite, which cuts the layers of the aura, or molybdenite, which mends them, when you push energy through pearl and coral, the layers of the aura become softer, more pliable, and porous. Ideally, the pulse of energy that you send through them should be vibrating or perhaps feel like a thrumming.

Why would you want to do this? If you are finding that it is difficult to extend and stretch out your aura, your subtle body, working with pearl or coral can help give you greater flexibility and range. If flexibility is not an issue, but absorbing and retaining unwanted energy patterns is a problem, then you can use these materials to ease their extraction. Using the pearl or coral to make your aura softer and more flexible makes it easier to release and draw out the unwanted energies. Almost any pearl or piece of coral will do so long as it is real. It does not have to be jewelry quality; the energy will be the same. For our purposes, do not use freshwater pearls because they are less effective.

Quartz

This entry is here primarily to remind you that quartz is the most easily programmed of minerals and that it would behoove you to have several prepared for your specific needs in your pouch of crystals.

Selenite

The mineral selenite comes in many forms and colors, but for the purposes described here, you need either the clear and translucent sheet-like version or the rod-like fiber-optic version. This is a fragile stone, so be cautious in how you transport it. Extended immersion in water can damage this mineral.

If you have a piece that is sheet-like and relatively clear, you can view through it to extend your psychic sight. Think of it as a filter that enables you to differentiate between *colors* that would otherwise look the same to you. As an example, this mineral makes it easier to see things in people's auras that should not be there but have camouflaged themselves. The same is true for scanning a landscape or room with selenite. The form of selenite that is more like fiber optics in appearance can help improve concentration for focusing your energy or perceptions. Selenite wands are also good for breaking up negative energy that is hanging in the air and other kinds of clearing away of the residue of difficult magick. The stone can also be used to open the upper chakras to a greater degree in preparation for communing with spirits, God/dess/es, and other similar practices. This mineral can be used as a visual focus for hypnosis, self-hypnosis, or trance work. Ideally, you would find both a sheet of selenite and a rod of selenite. A palm stone could also work.

Shungite

Information about the mineraloid shungite is readily available, so I focus on its less common uses here. Both molybdenite and shungite can heal injuries to the subtle bodies, but shungite is preferred because it also encourages recovery from the loss of life force and provides an orderly healing of the layers that were damaged. Shungite can also be used as a touchstone to determine the difference between healthy and unhealthy energy patterns in living beings and objects. It can help discern what is inherent and what is parasitic. The stone will often feel hotter and lighter when it is in contact with noxious things. This is a particularly valuable stone when seeking the truth from a less than reliable spiritual entity as a truth detector.

Star Diopside (Star of India)

The star diopside stone is mostly composed of the mineral diopside with a small amount of the mineral magnetite. As the star diopside forms, the fibers of magnetite align with the Earth's magnetic field, thus producing the four-rayed star that appears in star diopside. This stone carries the imprint of the Earth's aura in a very visible fashion. It is the most powerful of all the stones for grounding. It is useful in reconnecting people to the root of their incarnation, the source of their being. It facilitates both direct and map-based dowsing, and for that matter any exploration of the landscape, including the mapping of ley lines. It is my preferred stone for viewing changing weather patterns, ocean conditions, and deep earth energies. If you have received a strong emotional or psychic shock, star diopside helps give emotional release and revive your will to continue.

Stibnite

Stibnite is the mineral form of the metaloid antimony and is toxic if taken internally. Among its names in Alchemy are the Gray Wolf and the Black Dragon. This mineral does not increase your psychic abilities, but it can be an ally when things go wrong. Its greatest value is that it is like a scalpel or blade that can cut into the layers of the aura of both physical and nonphysical beings. Stibnite can be used in healing work that involves removing or extracting attached thought forms or beings. It can also be used to create an opening to insert something positive and useful. In addition, it can be used as a weapon. Another use is in the removal of workings, spells, and psychic imprints from physical objects such as small portable objects or even the walls of houses. Try to find pieces of stibnite that have a blade-like or rod-like appearance. The fan-shaped forms and clusters are of lesser use for these purposes.

Tiger Iron

Tiger Iron is not a single mineral; instead, it is a naturally occurring interweaving of tigereye, hematite, and red jasper. It has many uses, but it is most commonly used when you are having a hard time remaining clear and lucid, while in communication with a nonphysical being or in a divinatory trance. It does not sever or weaken your connection with spirits; rather, it provides enough grounding support while maintaining open psychic senses so that you aren't as overwhelmed. Another very important use for this crystal is in rituals to send back negative workings and curses. In combination with other techniques, it can be used to set up or strengthen shields and wards. It is not a comfortable stone for everyone to hold. People who are distressed by the stone will not be harmed by the discomfort because they often need it but are not clear enough to know what they need. Try to acquire a small piece that you can carry with you easily. A wand is also a good choice, if you can find one.

Yellow Jasper

Yellow jasper, or butterscotch jasper, is an aggregate of microscopic pieces of quartz, chalcedony, and other materials. It supports and strengthens the solar plexus and the core of your energy field, and it helps align you with your will. It can act like a compass to help you navigate the other realms and help engage the engine of memory more fully. It also provides protection during astral projection, shamanic journeys, dream-walking, and other forms of spirit travel by repelling unwanted energies.

CHAPTER 11

The Cord Ward

Introduction

About twenty years ago, I made my first trip to New Orleans, the place that has become my favorite vacation destination. I was somewhat unprepared for my second trip to New Orleans, however. My second trip was during the week of Halloween. At that time, the air was thick with magick from multiple layers of history's energy radiating from every place. The call of spirits was loud, since downtown you are never far from a graveyard, and there are countless people buried beneath the streets and sidewalks. I had partaken in several days and nights of sightseeing, nightclubs, and occult shenanigans; I had burned my candle at both ends and the middle. I was drained and staying in a hotel that had more than its share of ghosts. I was not bothered by all the bodiless visitors in the suite, but one of my traveling companions was more than a little spooked. Normally, I would have cleared the space and warded the room and proceeded with a good night's sleep, or what remains of one at 4 A.M. As it was, I was too tired and had a wee bit too much whiskey in my system to do the task well.

Necessity did prompt invention, and I came up with a ward that would work whether or not I was fully up to the task. I did have a vial of charged anointing oil and some sea salt in my luggage for a ritual I was doing in New Orleans, and my friend, the avid knitter, had some yarn. I cut a piece of yarn and tied the two ends together to make a loop big enough to go around my friend's bed. I mixed salt and water to make a thick brine and dipped the yarn into it. I squeezed out the excess and then put the oil on my palms and ran the entire loop through my hands, while pushing energy through them and into the yarn. I asked my friend to get into their bed, and I spread the loop on the floor around the bed. I envisioned the loop of yarn forming the boundary of a shield of light surrounding them from every direction. My friend slept, they awoke refreshed, and the first version of the Cord Ward was born. In a pinch, you can create much with very little. When I returned home from the trip, I continued to refine and strengthen the Cord Ward, which I share in this chapter. Of course, you can make a quick and easy Cord Ward, like my first one, but the more elaborate version can be reused and is more powerful.

Before continuing, I'd like to explain what I mean by wards and how they differ from shields in protective magick. A *ward* is a magickal construct that protects a specific place, a volume of space, such as a home, a room, an altar, and so on. A ward is empowered through ritual and/or the inherent properties of the materials or symbols that are used, and remains active, whether or not a practitioner is still actively supplying energy and control.

A *shield* surrounds a living being and it moves with that person, although it can be extended to include others. Shields are powered directly from the power of the person who created them, and some portion of that person's consciousness is allocated to the control and maintenance of the shield. Wards persist longer but have less flexibility of response than shields. Wards and shields can be used separately or combined to meet the needs of specific scenarios.

Uses

When you travel or are weary or do not have time to set up wards, you can quickly set up protection around yourself or others. The Cord Ward is not only helpful against spirits or spiteful intrusions, but also as a way to create a buffer against a loud or unsettled energetic environment. You may also use the Cord Ward if you need a spot of quiet to meditate or work on composing yourself. It is especially useful if you share your living space with others and need a quick and tidy way to create a safe space for your work. Also, you can give the Cord Ward to someone else who does not have the time or skill to protect themselves but is sensitive to these influences. I have given these as gifts to friends with sensitive children as well.

Components

Cord

You may use yarn, cord, or twine to create your Cord Ward. Thread is too prone to tangles and breakage. You must use a natural fiber, such as cotton, linen, or bamboo. Natural fibers take and hold energy, instructions, and intentions for much longer than artificial fibers. Plant-based fibers tend to be the best, though silk works very well. Wool seems to degrade over time after exposure to salt and oils and loses the charge faster than the other natural fibers I've tested. The length of the cord depends on how big an area it needs to cover. I suggest 9 yards (27 feet), which is enough to comfortably surround a king-size bed. You may adjust the length for a larger or a smaller Cord Ward, but you will also need to adjust the volume of the water and oils used to infuse the cord.

Brewing Water

1 teaspoon agrimony
2 medium bay leaves
3 cloves
1 teaspoon basil
1 teaspoon vervain
4 tablespoons sea salt
1-3 pieces of rusty iron such as nails; or scrape ¼ teaspoon of rust from an object
16 oz. water

Anointing Oil

9 drops frankincense oil
9 drops angelica root oil (may substitute with cedar)
½ oz. olive oil or almond oil

A Pouch

Large enough to hold the Cord Ward.

Optional

A small charm, bead, or pendant crystal.

Instructions for Creating the Ward

Put the herbs and minerals in a heat-proof glass or ceramic container. Next, rub your hands together briskly to open your Palm Chakras and place your hands over the dry ingredients. Then pour energy from your Palm Chakras onto the ingredients. By doing so, you are awakening the virtues that are in the herbs and instructing them with their purpose in the Ward. Do this until it feels that they are charged and awakened.

Bring water to a boil; then pour over the dry ingredients and let them steep for seven to nine minutes. Strain the brew into another glass or ceramic bowl and allow it to cool. Coil the cord into the brew and push it down so that it is all under water. If needed, use a plate smaller than the bowl to hold it down. Let it soak in the brew for at least ten minutes. Take out the cord and let it dry. If possible, let it dry outside under the sun. A clothesline is great if you have one.

When the cord is dry, knot it into a loop with three knots. If you wish, you may add a small charm, bead, or crystal pendant at the knot. Then hold the knot between your two palms and weave energy back and forth until the cord has become an energetic loop. Envision tiny fibers of energy that bind the knot so that from a magickal perspective there is no break between the two ends of the cord.

Then place the anointing oil in the palm of your right hand and grasp the cord in a loose grip. Use your left hand to pull the cord through widdershins (counterclockwise) while pushing energy into it and slowly intoning this spoken rune:

Back and Aback

Avaunt and Away

All Harm Stay Back

All Harm Away!

Continue until you feel that every part of the cord has been anointed. It is fine to pause to place more oil in your hand; just make sure the energy flow is consistent.

Once again, let the cord air dry for a day or two. If it is still too moist after that time, then dry it with a piece of cloth before putting it in the pouch.

Instructions for Using the Cord Ward

Setup

Take the cord from the pouch and spread it out so that it surrounds the area you intend to protect. It need not be a perfect circle, oval, square, or for that matter, any particular shape. I prefer placing it on the ground or floor, but that is not necessary and is not always possible. It does not need to be on a flat surface. If it must drape over tables, chairs, and so on, that is not a problem. It will form a bubble of protection based on the shape set by the cord. It will still work even if it is a bumpy and lopsided oval. When you're ready, step inside the loop of the cord. From inside the boundary of the cord, touch the cord and intone one to three times:

Back and Aback
Avaunt and Away
All Harm Stay Back
All Harm Away!

Visualize the bubble of protection surrounding you. If the ward is to protect multiple people, they should all be touching the cord as the rune is intoned. If you find it difficult to bend down to touch the Cord Ward, make sure that some part of it is draped at a height that is comfortable for you.

You and all who touched the cord may enter and exit the Cord Ward without disrupting it. If it is to be left up for more than a night's rest, then those who touched the Cord Ward should touch it and the rune once a day.

If the Cord Ward was a gift and you feel that the recipients may fumble or not remember the whole rune, as an alternative, tell them that they can touch the cord and intone one to three times:

All Harm Away!

They must visualize the bubble of protection.

Takedown

To take down the Cord Ward, touch the cord from inside and begin to wind it up from the inside to a size that will fit in the pouch. When you put it in the pouch, you should envision a bright glow inside the pouch. You may wish to take a breath and blow energy into the pouch as well. Finally, close the pouch with a knot.

Maintenance

Once every three or four months, depending on frequency of use, you should recharge the ward. Open the pouch but leave the cord inside. Now imagine that the air around you is teeming with sparks of life force. Take three deep breaths of the sparkling air; then take three more breaths and blow the sparkling air into the pouch. If you currently use some other method for pranic breathing, you may use it. Then intone once into the pouch:

Back and Aback
Avaunt and Away
All Harm Stay Back
All Harm Away!

Close the pouch with a knot and store it away. Once a year, re-anoint the cord using the oil and recharge it.

Some Variations

You may also use the materials and the idea of the Cord Ward in other ways. For example, you may use a rope or braided cords to created a protective cingulum, a belt that can be worn when doing healing work or other work that requires a barrier. It can also be used as a ward around altars or cabinets that contain your magickal gear. I have used smaller Cord Wards to tie together packages for storage or shipping that contained delicate magicks to protect them from degradation. You can use the anointing oil in combination with the Back-and-Aback spoken rune to protect doors, windows, and so on. Since you have created the oil and cords, you may as well use the remainders productively.

CHAPTER 12

Strengthening the Spiritual Immune System

Assuming you have a healthy immune system, for the most part, you don't catch a cold every time someone sneezes in your vicinity, nor does every minor scrape become infected. Similarly, when you spread forth your psychic senses and encounter something unwholesome, you do not automatically succumb to its influence. To extend this line of thought, when you touch a pernicious thought form, a miasma, it need not take up residence in your aura and strengthen or replicate itself.

In addition to your physical immune system, you also have a spiritual immune system that serves to protect you from patterns that will linger in your energy field. To be clear, this is something different from being affected by other people's emotions or energies, as was discussed in Chapter 5, "Managing Psychic Sensitivity." Your spiritual immune system's primary purpose is to maintain the template of your soul, the balance of qualities that make you uniquely yourself for this particular incarnation. A healthy spiritual immune system does not prevent changes; it disallows that which would be inharmonious or counter to your soul's evolutionary journey.

When I've introduced this concept in classes that I have taught, I have been asked whether or not having a weak or compromised physical immune system has an impact on the spiritual immune system. The answer to that question has many layers and is equal parts of yes and no. On the one hand, when you are stretched too thin, when you're exhausted, it is easier to become ill. And on the other hand, I have known people with many physical problems, inherent and/or acquired, whose spiritual power and fortitude were as bright as the noonday Sun. It is true that mind, body, and spirit are interconnected and have a profound impact on each other. And it is also true that people can have strengths and weaknesses, brilliance and mediocrity, woven together in a complicated braid. Almost every system and school has some variation on the phrase "know thyself" as one of its teachings. One of the outcomes of knowing yourself is that you know what needs your work and attention within yourself. Do what you can in all your parts and in every arena of your life that you can. Please do not believe that the limits that you have in some parts of your being spread and stretch equally into your other parts.

Just as there are methods to support the physical immune system, there are also methods to fortify the spiritual immune system. Aside from the obvious value of having a strong spiritual immune system to avoid impairment, knowing that you have a robust defense against otherworldly ailments will also improve your psychism. Feeling safer will enable you to open your senses more fully and deeply. In addition, the practices that strengthen the spiritual immune system also encourage a stronger connection between the Three Selves, which also smooths the way for subtle perception.

The Power of a Blessing

Just as good food, rest, and physical activity help strengthen the physical immune system, blessings help strengthen the spiritual immune system. This does not mean that you should go forth and seek the blessing of everyone and everything that seems appropriate. Blessings that others lay upon you are valuable, but when it comes to strengthening your spiritual immune system, the blessings that you call upon yourself are more profound. Like confidence, blessings are best when they come from within. Like calls to like, and when you contemplate the blessings that you have, more follow. I have four qualities that I often return to and work with through meditation, affirmation, and simple poems. I think of gratitude, caring, unity, and love as being the four vitamins that are essential for the spiritual immune system. Amplifying these four qualities within yourself will do much to prevent becoming tainted with many spiritual illnesses.

Gratitude

Quite a few studies have shown that recognizing and expressing gratitude have a positive impact on physical, emotional, and mental health. Formal and informal groups exist in the real world and in social media that provide support and encouragement for those doing gratitude practices. This is the easiest of the four qualities to begin with. In addition to gratitude for matters of the world, please consider expressing gratitude for experiences and gifts received through your spiritual experiences. Reflect on the marvel of your psychic senses and the expanded universe that they have given you. Think upon how grateful you feel for the times that you have received guidance or foreknowledge. Remember your emotions when you have thanked a spiritual entity for help or been thanked by others for your help.

Gratitude is the first and most important of these four qualities because the other three rest on its foundation. The expression of gratitude builds spiritual courage and the power to back up acts of courage.

Caring

Pay attention to how and when you express care and nurturing to others. To balance the scales, also pay attention to how others show care and nurturing to you. Consider the acts of kindness that you perform for friends, loved ones, strangers, animal companions, and so on. When you are in the presence of beings that you care for, become aware of how your viewpoint broadens to include their needs and their experience of their environment. When you have been the recipient of acts of caring, think on how the giver of that kindness knew to do so. Caring in all its forms, whether a physical or a spiritual act, increases our situational awareness in a positive way. The expression of caring builds spiritual vigilance and the discernment to know what is needed both when and where.

Unity

Everything in the Universe is one, and all things are interconnected. This is an oft-repeated core belief in many systems of magick, spirituality, and religion. Many have written and spoken of peak experiences wherein they undergo a moment of exaltation during which this unity is not a formulaic statement, it is a reality. The Universe is one but consists of many overlapping relationships and overlapping scales of magnitude. Unity is also experienced in smaller, more subtle ways as well. Feelings of being connected to others in everyday life, at a meal, a sporting event, a casual encounter while shopping, and so on, are all a manifestation of unity at a smaller scale. When you work on a task with others, when you do your part for the common good of a community, when you give your unique contribution to the world, you are an agent of unity. The mystery and the paradox of enmeshing yourself with your connections to the whole are that you become more clearly and distinctly aware of who you are and what part you play. The awareness and acknowledgment of unity, interconnectedness, build strong spiritual defenses and solidity of identity.

Love

Love contains portions of the qualities of gratitude, caring, and unity and is a far-reaching category that includes numerous kinds of emotions and states of being. Love can be very specific and focused, just as it can be broad and diffuse. Love can be personal, impersonal, and transpersonal. I believe that love in its highest sense is the equilibrating force that holds the Universe together. Love contains within itself the essence that brings forth loyalty, commitment, and the willingness to serve others both great and small. Love is omnidirectional; when it is directed outward, it also goes within, and when it is directed inward, it also radiates outwards. The tending and the fostering of love seek to establish harmony out of dissonance, and by so doing bring about healing.

Giving Permission

It is very likely that you acknowledge the existence of Divine beings, beneficent Spirits, or some other type of spiritual entity that works to help humanity. You may also have the expectation that these beings have your back and are offering you protection and assistance. One of my teachers once told me that one of the hallmarks of wise and benevolent beings is that they respect your free will, your capacity to act and to make choices. This means that an offer of protection is not the same as the acceptance of that offer. Unless you have explicitly requested their assistance, your tutelary beings may or may not act, depending on where they draw the line between intervening and interfering. I make it a practice to unequivocally ask for assistance and give permission to the God/des/es and other spirits that I work with on a regular basis, and reaffirm that permission before beginning psychic, spiritual, or magickal work. Depending on your preferences, you may consider this a prayer, an affirmation, or a conversation, but the gist of it is the same. If you would receive help, ask for it and graciously accept offers that are tendered.

Direct Methods for Reinforcing Spiritual Immunity

In this two-level technique, the first is a prerequisite for the second. They both offer protection from psychic or empathic overload, but more importantly, they protect the soul and spirit from infection, intrusion, and/or being controlled by an unwholesome force or entity. This method works through the activation of a lesser-known chakra and an endocrine gland that collectively form what I call the Root of the Spirit. Various lesser chakras and energy centers are named in Eastern and Western methodologies, and this is the one most suited to supporting the spiritual immune system. The human energy field and all its subtle bodies are more intricate than all the systems for describing it. Do not confuse the descriptions of the human energy field with its actual nature. You will find many variations on what I am describing, and I am not making the claim that what I am offering is the only or best approach. The technique that I am sharing here is one that I have developed, tested, and found effective.

For this technique you will be working with the Root of the Spirit, whose physical plane anchor is located on or just above the bump of the C7 vertebra of the neck (see illustration). This is the transition from the back to the neck on the spine. There are seven vertebrae in the neck, and the bottom one forms a prominent bump that you can easily find with your fingers. Energetically, the neck is like a higher octave of the back, and the lowest neck vertebra energy center acts like a higher octave Root Chakra. Unlike the chakras that you have probably studied, the primary placement for this one is on your backside, instead of your front side.

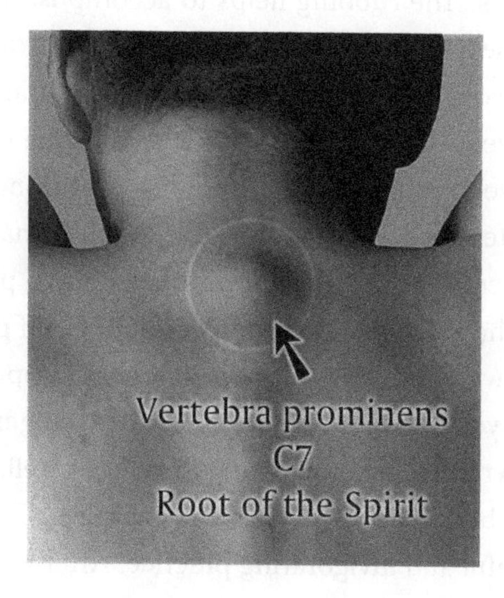

Like most significant energy centers in your subtle bodies, the Root of the Spirit is also attached to a gland or organ. In this case, it is the thymus, which is the gland responsible, among other things, for guiding the development of the T-cells in your immune system. This gland is large when we are young and shrinks as we age. It is above the heart, between the lungs, and behind the sternum. You may have heard of the practice of vigorously thumping the area over the thymus with three fingers as a holistic health practice to stimulate the physical immune system. The thymus is also the gland that governs parts of our spiritual immunity that discerns what is friend and what is foe. To use these techniques, you must become aware of the location of these two points in your anatomy, and you must awaken your energetic awareness of them as well.

Awakening Spiritual Immunity

Begin by rubbing your hands together and building up energy in your fingers. The rubbing helps to accomplish the build-up of energy in several ways. The sensations in the skin focus your attention on your hands, and energy follows your attention. The friction between the layers of your aura and the difference in polarity between your hands raise energy. Additionally, the rubbing stimulates blood flow to the hands, which makes it easier to access etheric energy. Then, after the rubbing, pat and push energy into the area on and around vertebra C7. If possible, feel and see the whirling energy of a small chakra opening there. Now thump your sternum with two or three fingers over your thymus center while pushing energy into it as well. Repeat this process until both places feel alive and energized. This, in and of itself, is a useful and invigorating practice. After you have a feel for this part, you can move on to the next step.

1. Envision a tube of light inside your body that connects your thymus gland near the front of your chest to your Root of the Spirit at the nape of your neck. The color of the energy can be white, brilliance, silver, or gold—whatever feels right to you.

2. Now breathe in life force through your thymus center and exhale it through your Root of the Spirit. Repeat this flow of energy from the center of your chest to the nape several times.
3. Then reverse the direction of the process and breathe in life force through your Root of the Spirit and exhale it through your thymus center. Repeat this flow of energy from the nape to the thymus center of your chest several times. If you are feeling good, you can continue to the next step. If anything feels amiss, that is enough for the day, and you should start the process over again the next day.
4. Now alternate between inhaling and exhaling energy through each center. Complete a cycle of energy respiration, inhale and exhale, at the thymus; then complete a cycle with the Root of the Spirit and continue. Continue until you feel that the pattern of moving energy back and forth between the two centers is well established. Normally, this process takes about two to three minutes, after which you can cease your efforts.

The enhanced spiritual immunity generated by the activation of these centers will begin to drop off sharply in one to two hours and then fade slowly over four to five more. When used as a regular practice, this process has a long-lasting strengthening effect on your spiritual immunity.

The Helm of Light

After you have been working with the Spiritual Immunity technique for a while and have comfort and ease with its use, you may try the Helm of Light. I generally use this technique only when I know that I am about to take part in activities that are risky.

1. Start with the process described in the preceding section, "Awakening Spiritual Immunity."

2. Begin by envisioning that with each breath of the life force that you take in, your thymus center and your Root of the Spirit are sending out energy to form a bubble, a Helm of Light, that is anchored to those two centers. Think of the shape of an old deep-sea diver's helmet as a general guide. The top of the Helm of Light should be over your Crown Chakra, but not over your Transpersonal/Personal Kether. In other words, the Helm should be below the outermost edge of your aura. Do not draw on energy from your other chakras to create the Helm, especially the Crown Chakra, because this would narrow the range and frequencies of the shield.

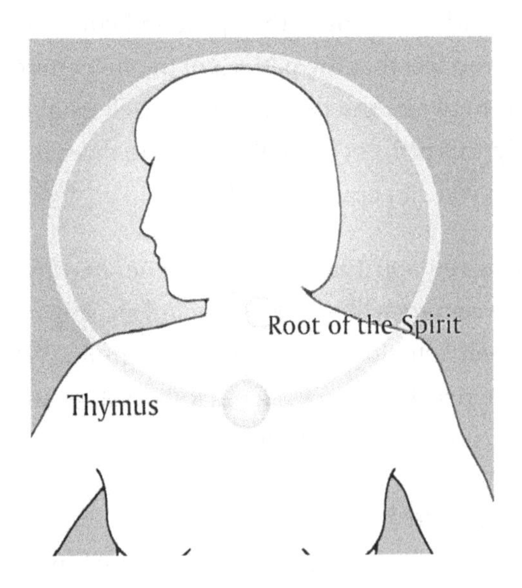

3. When you no longer need the enhanced protection, release the Helm by reabsorbing the energy at your thymus center and your Root of the Spirit. Then ground and center as needed, and close down your psychic senses.

Most people find it hard to maintain the Helm for more than an hour, with two or three hours being the maximum limit. After you use this technique, it is a good idea to have something to eat to replenish yourself.

CHAPTER 13

Skrying Methods

The term *skrying,* also spelled *scrying,* is often applied to a wide assortment of practices that involve gazing at an object to receive psychic impressions or messages. Some use the term *skrying* so broadly as to include methods that require no physical object. From my perspective, that is not skrying, although it may be a form of divination or the mantic arts. The disciplines, rituals, and protocols for skrying are incredibly diverse and are constantly being expanded and modified because it is a living art. For many, the mention of skrying calls up images of the classic fortune-teller with a crystal ball or perhaps of Galadriel in *The Lord of the Rings* pouring water into a basin to see far and wide. Since accounts of skrying traditions appear in many cultures over many centuries, a comprehensive study of the art would need to be broken up into many volumes arranged by time period and culture. This chapter focuses on what I have assembled as the core concepts and praxes, which are readily learned.

The essence of skrying is in the use of a physical surface to externalize inner psychic perceptions. A surface for skrying may be solid, such as that of a crystal or mirror. A surface for skrying may also be changeable, such as a liquid, smoke, or a flame. In fact, any of the Four Elements or a combination of them may provide the target for externalized psychism. An object that is appropriate for skrying may be as refined and ornate as a beveled mirror in an ornate gold-leafed frame, a faceted gem set in a ring, or as simple and rustic as red clay set with a rain puddle reflecting the sky. There are many traditional implements for skrying:

- Standard mirrors, black mirrors, or polished metal mirrors
- Glass or quartz spheres, natural crystals with large flat areas, or faceted stones
- Flames from candles, lamps, or hearths
- Smoke from smoldering herbs or resins in a brazier or a wood fire
- Fluids in bowls, basins, or cups
- Natural objects, such as puddles, ponds, or stones in a landscape

This list is a good start. It does not give all the possibilities, but it does indicate the range of options. There is no such thing as the best tool for skrying; finding the right tool for you is a matter of individual needs, temperament, and sometimes the nature of the question or the environment of the moment.

I have had students tell me that they can't skry, that they've tried this practice more than once and it didn't work for them. While it is true that skrying isn't for everyone, it has been my experience that many of the less-than-satisfactory skrying attempts are due to using a surface or a technique that does not match the individual or the specific work at hand. Also, although the classic stereotype is that the skryer *sees* images, it may be that you will hear, feel, or sense more than you see when you skry. The only way to discover which forms of skrying work for you is through experimentation and through the keeping of good notes on your efforts. The following sections describe some of the general parameters to explore.

Outer, Inner, Through

I owned an occult shop for a decade, and I had many customers who would come in looking for a skrying mirror or a crystal ball. To help them narrow down their choices, I would often begin by determining which depth of focus, partly physical and partly metaphysical, they preferred. Some people have a tendency to focus on the outer surface of their skrying tool. Others let their focus sink below the outer surface into the material itself. Some have a focus that passes through the skrying tool completely. A few people have a predisposition to change their focus several times during the same skrying session. A black glass skrying mirror would not be a good fit for someone whose focus is within the material. In this case, a crystal ball or a bowl filled with liquid may be better. Skrying into a flame or smoke is more suitable for people whose focus moves through or shifts during their efforts. Be mindful of how you look and how you focus your gaze when skrying, and take note of how you respond to the optical qualities of the tool or material that you are using. Over time you'll establish which sorts of materials work well with your style.

Tone and Color

Another variable to consider in your preferences is the tone and color of the material. Some people may find that they do best with a black or dark material for skrying; others find that a white or pale material is better for them. I have had to dissuade people who were making no progress at all from choosing black mirrors or obsidian spheres just because their friends or teachers preferred them; that doesn't mean that those tools would also be their best choice. For certain people, a white or pale surface acts as a better screen onto which they can project their inner sight. For the most part, monochromatic surfaces are favored, but some individuals find that they are more effective when the surface has a distinct color. The choice of a color or colors is idiosyncratic. For example, although I do well with most skrying tools, I have a bowl that has swirls of dark blue and violet that works particularly well for me when filled with water.

Detailed or Plain

You may find that it is easiest for you to skry onto a surface that is perfectly uniform, without variation. In this case, an exceptionally clear quartz or glass sphere may be worth the extra expense. It is also possible that you may find that a busy, detailed material is a better choice. I find that crystals with many veils, flashes, and inclusions yield better results for me. If your inclination is for highly detailed materials, it is generally better to avoid something that has clearly identifiable shapes that will override your projected visions. If every time you look at the surface you see a marking that looks like a cat or a tree or a house, this may become problematic. Unlike reading the tarot, where some of the guidance comes from seeing an existing image in a new light or seeing it shift beneath your gaze, skrying requires a more neutral medium to allow your visions to become predominant. There are exceptions to any rule, but I leave that to your explorations.

Formal or Fast and Free?

The literature on skrying tends to concentrate on skrying mirrors and often elaborate procedures and rituals for both their creation and their use. A number of these methods take days or weeks of preparation, including astrological timing. There are also quite a few voices that argue for the value of the time and costly or rare materials in these measures. They are quite right to extol the worth of investing time and effort in these matters. Nonetheless, in a pinch, I have skryed successfully in a mug filled with black coffee in a hotel restaurant. Would I have liked to have had my consecrated obsidian mirror instead? My answer is yes, but it was at home in my cabinet of ritual tools. The answer to whether or not to take a formal approach or to fly by the seat of your pants is frequently determined by circumstances.

In actuality, the tools or rituals you use are on more of a continuum of practices and choices rather than being either/or situations. So, in addition to the needs of pragmatism, it is important to find your comfort zone between these two poles. You could also conceptualize this spectrum as pure ritual and pure psychism, which is a partially true description. Your style of magick and/or psychism may not map well onto this pattern. If you are averse to formality and ritual, I ask that you try to include more ritual elements in your skrying. If you are wary of spur-of-the-moment skrying without all the bells and whistles, let your psychism be your preparation. The goal is to be confident and competent regardless of the state of affairs. The value of a well-charged and -maintained skrying tool is that it can amplify and clarify visions while maintaining a protective boundary for the skryer. However, the skrying tool cannot provide talent and training; that is the up to the skryer.

Preparations for Skrying Tools

Whether or not you are purchasing or making a skrying tool, I recommend that you purify it before using it. This cleansing can be simple or extensive, and the suggestions I offered in Chapter 10, "Working with Minerals," apply here as well. Even in impromptu skrying, such as in a mug of black coffee, there is enough time to flush energy through the object to make it clear and ready for use.

It is also a good idea to cleanse skrying tools periodically as needed. You can buy, make, or repurpose objects to become skrying tools, as dictated by your interests, budget, and crafting skills. I find that you can achieve better results when the skrying tool is consecrated and set aside for only the purpose of skrying. In this case, consecration involves the imprinting of your intention and purpose onto the tool. If you have a specific religious or spiritual path, you may wish to ask for the tool to be blessed and supported by the forces and beings related to that path.

If certain symbols or sigils are meaningful to you, you may wish to place them on the skrying tool. You can create a visible mark reinforced with energy or an invisible one inscribed in energy alone. Symbols can also be derived from natural sources. I have a friend who has a special connection to spiders and spider webs. She has a skrying bowl on whose back she caught a spiderweb, which she then varnished in place. The more you personalize a skrying tool, the more effective it will be for both energetic and psychological reasons.

The Process of Skrying

Begin by creating sacred space, an energetic container for the work. This may be accomplished with words, visualization, and/or physical actions. The primary purpose for creating sacred space before skrying is to reduce distractions, interruptions, and interference. Although such use is rare, sometimes it is also for protection. For some, it is enough to invoke your connection and alignment with spiritual forces. Perhaps you'll want to visualize a circle or sphere of light surrounding you, with or without the recourse of physically scribing the circle. It may be that what suits you better is the model of the sacred crossroads or the World Tree for the setting of sacred space. For some, the image of being enfolded in the wings of an angel or a Goddess is the right choice. Let the style and the intensity of the establishment of sacred space match your aesthetics and the nature of the work.

Then shift deeper into the state of being that brings your psychic senses into the foreground of your consciousness. You may wish to do some of the warm-up exercises that were shared earlier in this book. Reach out and connect your energy to the skrying tool until you feel that it has meshed with your aura. You may wish to make passes with your hands over the tool as a method of strengthening this connection. Since you will be externalizing your psychic senses onto the skrying tool, the strength of connection from the tool to your aura has a strong impact on the quality of your perceptions.

The next step is to open the portal of the surface of the tool; this is both a psychological action and a magickal/energetic action. My preferred approach starts with taking a deep breath and closing my eyes. I let my eyes relax for a moment; then I flutter my lids open to look on the surface of the tool, and I part the veil of the Earth plane. You can part the veil by passing your hands over the surface, scribing a symbol such as a spiral or invoking pentacle, or blowing it away with an energized breath, visualization, or any method that appeals to you. Lastly, envision a portal, a frame of energy that will hold open the veils that you have parted. The goal here is to have the frequency, the focal point plane of reality, of the surface of the skrying tool be a match to those of your inner senses.

This is the time when you should pose a question or a request for guidance, when you should engage the engine of memory. The intention to view a specific time or place also qualifies as a question. I do not recommend completely open-ended skrying unless you are a talented and experienced skryer. Without a directive, skrying is more likely to show you fantasy, information from your subconscious, half-truths from mischievous beings, and so on. You can ask more than one question during the same skrying session without starting over. Start with short sittings at first so that you don't drift off task during a session, and build up to longer skrying durations.

When you are done, close down the skrying tool to close the portal. Push the veils back into place so that the surface is fully enclosed in the Earth plane. Pull in your aura, your energy, so that you are no longer enmeshed with the energy of the skrying tool. Offer thanks and gratitude for whatever information you received. Release and dismiss whatever construct you used to create sacred space, bounded space. Take a few breaths and then return to your normal state of consciousness. Dial down your psychic senses and ground and center if needed. Write down your impressions as a precaution against your memories of the session fading. If others were present with you, collect their impressions as well.

Tips and Troubleshooting

Following is a collection of suggestions for experimentation, ways to improve your skrying practices, and techniques to move past obstacles that may hinder your efforts. The recipes for some expansions on the suggestions are shown later in Chapter 14, "Herbs, Oils, and Potions for Psychic Work."

Bowls, Basins, and Such

Water is the most commonly used liquid placed into vessels used for skrying. You may wish to darken the water using ink or food coloring. If you're using a small vessel, pure India ink is as good as an obsidian mirror. Experiment with the level of opacity and color of the water in addition to that of the vessel.

I have found red wine or wine mixed with water to be an excellent medium for skrying. You may also wish to brew a potion of visionary herbs and use it instead of plain water. If your skrying is enhanced by a busy, detailed surface, consider pouring a small quantity of heavy cream into the water while posing your question. Blow on the cream or give it a gentle stir with a fingertip and then skry into the swirls. You may also use oils as a substitute for cream. Combinations of oils and herbs that are mixed specifically for this purpose are called Skryer's Milk.

Crystal Balls

I have heard many partisans argue that glass spheres are useless and that quartz or natural mineral spheres are the only way to go. Oddly enough, many of these same people have no quibbles about black glass mirrors. I prefer natural crystal spheres because I take advantage of the fact that the mineral will hold programming and a charge better than glass. However, these sorts of spheres can be expensive, which means you may need to buy smaller spheres. My experience is that for many people, the larger the sphere, the easier it is to use for skrying. Since glass or reconstituted quartz spheres are often cheaper, they may be a better choice.

The base or stand that is used to support a crystal ball is often neglected but should be considered part of the skrying tool. You can charge, consecrate, ornament, and modify the base or stand to uphold the work that you do with the crystal ball.

Fire and Smoke

If you are using a candle or an oil lamp or some other source of a single flame, try focusing on different parts of the flame to find which is best for you. Many find the darker, sometimes bluish, portion of the flame that is nearest to the wick to be the best portal. Or you may find that another place is your sweet spot. I prefer a relatively still flame, so I often place a glass cylinder around the candle. You may wish to dress (anoint) the candle with a spiritual oil blend before using it for skrying. If you are using an oil or alcohol lamp, you may wish to add a drop of an essential oil into the fuel to add specific energies to the flame.

Skrying into a fireplace, campfire, or other larger multiflame source is very different from looking into a single flame. Take some time to get to know the nature of that particular fire and tentatively extend your energy out to it until you find a resonant spot. Where your energy connects the most strongly is where you'll achieve good results. You may find yourself looking into the coals and wood as much as the fire itself. I often throw a handful of herbs or resins into a fire at the beginning and the end of a skrying session to open and then close the portal.

Not too many people prefer skrying in smoke, but if you do, please consider ventilation, safety, and the oft-forgotten smoke alarm. Successful smoke skrying generally requires thick, billowing smoke to act as a projection screen for your psychism. When I have done smoke skrying, it has been outdoors, or on a porch or in a gazebo. Indoors is fine, providing you have the right circumstances. The simplest method is to smolder herbs or resins on the charcoals used for incense or hookahs. Try using either dittany of Crete, fumitory, or gum arabic as single ingredients that produce thick smoke with good energy properties for skrying.

Mugwort Infusion Wash

Whether as a preparatory step or as a part of regular maintenance, washing your skrying tools in an infusion made with mugwort helps make for clearer visions. Brew a teaspoon of mugwort in two cups of hot water for five minutes. Strain the mixture and let it cool to a comfortable temperature. Then wash your crystal balls, mirrors, bowls, and so on with the mugwort infusion. You may dry them, but do not rinse off the infusion with water.

Lighting and Optics

If you are not having the results that you want, consider adjusting the lighting in the room or the angle at which the skrying tool catches the ambient light. More often than not, a dimmer room is better for skrying. If you can't change the lighting in the room, try skrying with your lids partly closed.

Get closer to the surface of the tool. Regardless of what your physical eyesight prefers as a focal distance, skrying is easier when the surface fills a significant portion of your visual field. If necessary, pick up the skrying tool with your hands, or if that is not practical, place it on a small stand.

Skrying by candlelight is a time-honored tradition for both the atmosphere and the energy that candles provide. There is also a charm to knowing how to arrange the candles. If you are using a mirror, ball, or bowl, place one candle to the left and another to the right of the tool. Move the candles toward you and/or further left or right until when you stare forward at the skrying tool, the candles are right on the edge of your peripheral vision. Then light the candles and proceed with your skrying session. For reasons I have yet to fathom, this technique tends to brighten and sharpen the skrying. A more advanced version of this approach involves placing the candles at your blind spots, which is even more effective but requires that you stay relatively still during the session. To do this, start by placing one candle 3 inches to the left and another 3 inches to the right of the tool. Both candles should be about 3 inches forward or backward from the tool. Face the skrying tool with your nose pointed to the center of the tool. Cover your left eye and focus on the left candle. Move your head closer and then farther away until the candle on the right vanishes. Take note of the distance that your head is from the tool because that is the optimal distance for viewing. You may need to experiment with the starting positions for the various items to find the most comfortable arrangement.

Warming Up

In addition to the various methods for opening the psychic senses that have been shared, two others are more specific to skrying. To do the first one, you should be outdoors or near a window so that you can look at the sky or a distant feature in the landscape. Hold a finger close enough to your face so that it is as close as it can be and still remain in focus. Next, quickly alternate your gaze between your finger and a distant point. Continue alternating between nearest and farthest focus until you feel a change in your eyes. This may take twenty seconds, or it make take two minutes. Let your sensations be your guide. Then proceed with your skrying session.

At times, you may become stuck and feel blocked in your skrying. Here is a method to overcome the friction and inertia and get your impressions flowing again. Obtain a sheet of paper, a card, a tile, or any other object that can be propped up and is a vibrant, solid color. It can be any of the seven colors of the rainbow, though I personally find yellow or orange to be the most fruitful for me. The lighting in the room should be bright, but you should be able to dim it quickly. A desk or table lamp will make this easier. Hold or prop up the brightly colored object and stare at it, blinking as little as possible for at least thirty seconds. Then dim the lights and turn your gaze to your skrying tool. An afterimage that is the complementary color of the object that you fixated on will appear in the skrying tool. This afterimage is a projection caused by the quirks of the retina's neurology, but it is an inner state projected outward, which starts the ball rolling for actual skrying.

Skrying in Nature

I am convinced that the first skrying took place in surfaces made by nature—lakes, ponds, puddles, tidal pools, wherever and whenever the water was still enough. In the 1980s when I lived in Wilmington, Delaware, I used to go down to the Brandywine River, which I lovingly called the Baranduin, to a large flat stone in the river that had an oval hollow in its center. The hollow in the stone would fill with water and be still while the river rushed around the large stone. I would sprawl across the stone and skry into the quiet spot in the middle of roaring waters. The time I spent skrying there greatly improved my ability to skry into tools made by people. Where I live now, there is a tree whose trunk and gnarled roots form a skrying basin that I use after it has rained enough. I encourage you to find a spot in nature to skry as an aid to developing your skrying skills and sensitivities.

CHAPTER 14

Herbs, Oils, and Potions for Psychic Work

The use of herbs, oils, and potions to enhance spiritual and psychic pursuits is a time-honored tradition. Many wonderful resources are available if you are interested in adding these practices to your repertoire. In this chapter, I share some insights and some recipes to help you start or add to what you have already collected. The recipes included here have been safe and efficacious for my students and me. However, everyone reacts differently to these materials, and allergies can be unpredictable, so be cautious with these or any other recipes you may encounter. Also, not every source of materials is reliable, accurate, or fresh. When I owned a metaphysical shop, I had several occasions when suppliers shipped me mislabeled herbs or resins, stale herbs, rancid oils, or material contaminated by the admixture of a second material. I could tell the difference, but some cannot. I suggest that you get to know the look, feel, and smell of the materials so that you'll be able to judge for yourself. If you have doubts about a material, don't use it. Even if it is safe, your doubt will have a negative impact on your use of it. Despite these warnings—and my allergies—I cannot imagine abstaining from the use of these materials in my work.

Many people have allergies or sensitivities that give them very good reasons to avoid exposure to incense, oils, and the like. Here, I start by offering suggestions on how to use the virtues of these materials without setting off a bout of misery. If you are not reactive, you will gain a lot as well because the information on tuning in to the energies of these materials is often overlooked. I also suggest some accommodations that can be made if you are working in a group with people who have allergies or sensitivities.

Herbs, resins, oils, and such—the materia of magick—work on us through three key modes: energetic, psychological, and biochemical. The energetic, or spiritual, power of the materials we use in this context comes from their origin; herbs, resins, and most of the oils come from living things. All living things are endowed with spiritual virtues and powers.

Energetic Effects

The energy patterns and spirit of the materials, with their unique combination of Elements, astrological imprints, life-stream, and so on, can have an effect on the atmosphere of the room that you are in and a direct effect on your aura. You can benefit from the energy of these materials without having to take them into your body by breathing them, anointing your skin, or ingesting them. How much assistance you receive from the energy of the materials depends on the work you do to awaken them and how well you tune in to them.

Awakening and Reconnecting

Let's say that you have some mugwort (*Artemisia vulgaris*) that you intend to use as part of a wash, a potion, incense, and so on.

If you have the good fortune of knowing where some is growing, then go to a living plant and become familiar with its energy. If not, then look up some pictures of the plant and reach out and try to connect with it. The aim is to have a sense of the power of the living spirit, the group soul, of mugwort. Then take some mugwort and put it in a small bowl, or leave it in a sealed container if you are allergic, and hold it in your hands. Feel the power of life coursing into the dried herb. Imagine a mugwort plant with its roots drawing life from the Earth and taking in light from the Sun. Remind yourself and the dried herb that it is still mugwort and that it is still connected to the flow of life of all mugwort. Draw some energy in through your Heart or Solar Plexus Chakra and push that energy into the mugwort. It is then ready to be used or added to a mixture.

Follow the same process with all your materials. When you're combining several materials, as you stir them, infuse the mixture with energy with the intent of unifying their virtues for the purpose at hand. If you are using a spoon or rod, imagine it to be a wand. I often charge up my hand and mix the herbs and resins directly.

Instructing and Consecrating

Although it is true that the materials have specific effects that have proven themselves to be consistent over time, most of the materials you are likely to utilize have more than one use. After you awaken the materials, it is a good idea to let them know what requests and instructions you have for them. It is prudent to treat the materials as living spirits and to let them know which of their virtues are being called into action. Words are good, but visualizations are often better in conveying your requests. Should you be mixing together enough of a blend so that you will be using it on more than one occasion, I recommend blessing it and consecrating it. This will help preserve some of the work that you have done until it is used again. It is always a good idea to freshen up the energy of a mixture before using it again.

Allergy Workarounds

For people who cannot burn incense, ingest potions, or use anointing oils, after you have prepared the materials, their energies and spiritual virtues are available to be used with a few adjustments. A bowl on the altar, filled with herbs and resins, can still fill a room with their energies without being burned. Hold your hand over the bowl and move your fingers imploringly to draw the energy up out of the bowl. Pull the energies upward and then spread them around the room.

Another option is to place the materials in a glass jar (resins are best for this), and shake the jar like a rattle as you walk about the room spreading the energies. If you have a potion that you cannot drink but would like its energetic benefit, brew it with a quartz crystal and let the herbs and the stone steep together. Pour out the liquid and herbs and save them as an offering to be poured out on the ground. Dry the crystal and then hold in and drink in the energies and pattern that it has absorbed. A pouch of herbs and resin in your pocket or around your neck on a string is also an excellent way to take in their power. When you use some imagination, allergies and sensitivities need not prevent you from having access to the magickal power of herbalism.

Psychological Effects

Every step in the process of collecting, preparing, and using these materials helps shift your mood and state of mind toward opening your inner senses. As you grind with your mortar and pestle, you can think on the work you will be doing. As you measure and mix ingredients, you can begin to focus on your intentions. Even waiting for the water to boil while making a potion can be part of a contemplative practice, whether you are quiet, humming, or chanting. The tongs you use to hold charcoal that you light for incense are conduits to charge the charcoal with your power and purposes.

Your sense of smell reaches deep into your memories, mind, and instinctual responses. Fragrances have the capability to move us from one state of consciousness to another. Many of the materials used for spiritual purposes work even if you haven't awakened their energies because of the power of their fragrance. There is also a trance-inducing quality to the smoke rising from a censer. Following the swirls and whorls of smoke with your eyes can also be a part of the process of opening the psychic senses. In addition to the scent and the touch on your skin, the steps you take in applying anointing oil on yourself, candles, crystals, and the like can become a ritual that moves you to a more open state of being.

Biochemical Effects

There has not been as much scientific research as there should be into the chemistry and mechanisms of action of plant materials used in spiritual work. Not surprisingly, when it has been done, this research often confirms the traditional teachings. In 2008, the *Federation of American Societies for Experimental Biology Journal* (commonly called the *FASEB Journal*) published an article that found that incensole acetate, one of the constituents in frankincense, lowers anxiety, elevates moods, and encourages a sensation of warmth. Other studies have produced similar conclusions, though they are still uncertain on the mechanism of action. Frankincense, in spiritual circles, is said to be an herb associated with the Sun, the Element of Fire, and is said to raise the vibration of a space. All these associations are symbolically congruent with the experimental studies. For a variety of political, monetary, and ideological reasons, science does not invest much effort into the study of spiritual claims; nonetheless, I encourage you to stay on the lookout for studies related to the materials that we use.

Although most of the plant materials in current use for spiritual purposes have a long history of safe use, individuals react differently and respond at different dosage levels. Be cautious as you explore the uses of herbs, resins, and oils. Additionally, if you are on medications, are pregnant, or have a known health condition, please consult with a health-care practitioner. Anything that works is likely to have some side effect or unplanned consequence. I suggest that you use the small amounts and low concentrations of most plant materials. For example, white sage is often smoldered to cleanse a space of harmful energies. By the way, it has also been shown to have antimicrobial properties. When I use white sage, it has to be in low concentrations; otherwise, I wake up the next day with my eyes crusty with sleep and irritation. Essential oils are extremely potent and highly concentrated. Use essential oils *only* after they have been diluted in a carrier oil or alcohol. You will find abundant literature on the use of all these materials, and I encourage you to educate yourself if you want to do more with them.

The Recipes

Following are a few of my recipes that I believe are a good starting point. When you make these recipes, be sure that you label the jars or vials and store them in a cool, dark place. Consider always keeping a little bit from each previous batch to add to the new batch. This practice helps build the strength and continuity of the energy and instructions that you have placed into the materials. I keep a small archival jar of each of my favorite recipes to ensure that I always have a link back to the original batch. It is a simple enough practice, and I have found that it produces real results.

I encourage you to create your own recipes from scratch or modify these or other recipes you may find. You may have better luck with your creations if you get to know the materials as single notes before you combine them into a melody. Try frankincense by itself, then jasmine blossoms, or lavender flowers, or mugwort, and so on, while taking note of how you respond to each.

Incense

Good brands of stick incense are available, especially the ones that are resin and oils on a stick, but nothing compares to the burning of incense on charcoal. Burning incense this way does take more planning and time, but the results are well worth the effort. This style of burning incense gives you more opportunities to energize the materials and add another layer of psychological connection. Be advised that a little bit of a resin goes a long way. Resins, such as frankincense and copal, are crystalized sap and highly concentrated. You will be astonished by how much smoke arises from one chunk of resin. When you burn incense, each particle of smoke filling the air is resonating with the spiritual power of the materials and rebroadcasting the intentions that you set within the incense.

If you are not allergic to the materials but are easily irritated by smoke, you can still get similar benefits by placing the materials in a container of boiling water. The steam that rises from the water will also carry the fragrance and the energy throughout the room. It is a great use for that fondue set that has been languishing in the cupboard. If you find that this method appeals to you, a wide arrange of decorative oil warmers and potpourri warmers can be used for this purpose. It is also useful if you are in a place that forbids incense but allows fragrances.

Second Sight Incense

⅛ teaspoon amber or amber resin
1 teaspoon copal resin
1 teaspoon dittany of Crete
½ teaspoon dragon's blood resin
1 teaspoon jasmine blossoms
2 teaspoons myrrh resin
1 teaspoon opoponax resin

Burn a small quantity of this incense on charcoal to awaken all your psychic senses, but sight in particular. Amber resin is not amber, but a combination of oils and resins that produce a similar fragrance and energy. I prefer real amber in this incense. If you do not have a source for real amber for incense, consider buying a low-quality amber chunk necklace and grind a bead as needed. If you are using powdered dragon's blood, use a bit less. Opoponax is often hard to find but well worth the search.

Smoke of Presence Incense

1½ teaspoons dittany of Crete
1 teaspoon elemi resin
½ teaspoon frankincense resin
½ teaspoon fumitory
½ teaspoon myrrh resin
1½ teaspoons opoponax resin
¼ teaspoon wormwood

This incense has two uses: as a smoke suitable for skrying and as an incense to facilitate communication with spirits. As you may gather, if it is suitable for skrying, it also requires ventilation because the smoke is very thick. If you are using it for working with the spirits, you need only a small pinch. Dittany of Crete is sometimes difficult to obtain; I encourage you to search because it truly is amazing. If you truly cannot find this plant, then substitute Greek oregano because it is a distant cousin, but keep looking for the dittany.

Keep It Simple Incense

1 teaspoon frankincense resin
1 teaspoon myrrh resin

You got me... this is hardly a recipe, but it is simple enough to remove the excuse that there were too many ingredients to track down. Give this a try, as a way to prove the value of this style of working with incense. After you use this two-ingredient classic combination, I am fairly certain you'll be encouraged to do more.

Oils

Although you can order all the essential oils and carrier oils that you need online, you may want to see if you have a local shop in your area. It may be an occult shop, a health food store, a holistic health center, a food co-op, a spa, or any of several other possibilities because oils are used in many practices. Do not assume that there are no resources in your area; ask around and search on the Internet. In addition to the convenience of a local resource, often shops will mix a recipe for you. By the ounce, a mixed recipe will often cost more, but the total outlay of money will be less. When and if you decide that you want to do more with oils, you will want to purchase in bulk quantities. As a first step, find your preferred carrier oil. This is easier if you can go to a shop and see what each oil feels like on your skin. Sweet almond oil is popular. One of my favorites is fractionated coconut oil, but you may prefer shea butter, grapeseed oil, olive oil, or one of the dozens of other possibilities.

Remember to awaken and prepare the oil for spiritual use. You can apply a few drops of oil to places such as the locations of the Third Eye, the Inner Ears, the pulse points of the hands, the Palm Chakra, or the Heart Chakra. Avoid getting the oil on your lips, and if you choose to anoint the Third Eye, make it just a touch of the oil, less than a drop. You do not want the oil from your brow spreading on your sweat and burning your eyes. Remember to wash your hands when you're done. You can also use these oils for anointing candles, skrying tools, crystals, or other objects that you may be using as adjuncts to your practices.

See Far—Hear Deep Oil

1 oz. sweet almond oil or some other carrier oil

Add these essential oils to the carrier:

5 drops clary sage
4 drops jasmine
2 drops lotus (white or pink 10% dilution)
3 drops myrrh
2 drops nutmeg
4 drops rosewood
3 drops vetiver

You can substitute with honeysuckle or tuberose if lotus is not available. Lotus oil is expensive and is often sold diluted. The two crucial ingredients in this recipe are clary sage and jasmine; in a pinch, other ingredients may be left out.

This oil, which has a longer-lasting effect than most, is used to open all the inner senses. Your psychic senses are likely to remain stimulated and more open for several hours after application. If you are highly sensitive, you may wish to add additional carrier oil.

Mantle of Light Oil

1 oz. sweet almond oil or some other carrier oil

Add these essential oils to the carrier:

4 drops amber (real amber, ideally)
3 drops angelica root oil (10% dilution)
2 drops cedar
3 drops frankincense
3 drops myrrh
2 drops peppermint
2 drops rock rose (aka labdanum, 10% dilution)

Depending on circumstances, anoint affected chakras, pulse points, and so on. This oil helps people connect with whatever inherent spiritual support they have. Use a simple prayer, affirmation, or chant while anointing them.

Skryer's Milk

Either pour carefully or use a dropper or a spoon to drop a small amount of the Skryer's Milk into a water-filled skrying vessel. Take an energized breath and softly blow across the surface and speak your intention before you begin.

My Recipe

¾ oz. coconut oil, ideally, or some other carrier oil
1½ oz. vodka, gin, or some other clear alcohol
1 bay leaf

Mix these well and then add a bay leaf, and let it steep overnight before removing it. Then add these essential oils to the mix:

6 drops star anise or fennel
4 drops cypress (optional)
3 drops myrrh (optional)

With the optional ingredients, you normally use one but not both. They are a bit of a bother to mix in but well worth their addition for the energy they add. The texture and color added by either of these oils also improve visions.

¼ teaspoon cascarilla (eggshell powder)

This ingredient adds a protective barrier against spirits and negative energy if the skrying you are about to undertake is risky. You can grind your own eggshells to a fine powder or buy cascarilla at a botanica or online.

¼ teaspoon white chalk powder

Take a piece of white chalk (or a white pastel stick) and break it in half. Use one half to write a name or a phrase, or draw a symbol that connects to the matter of your next skrying session on a small chalkboard or a piece of slate. Take the remaining half of the stick and grind it into powder that you mix into the Skryer's Milk. After the skrying session is over, erase the slate, but keep the chalk and the Skryer's Milk for your next endeavor.

Potions

The first thing that comes to mind when people hear the word *potion* is some magickal liquid that is drunk to achieve some change of state in their consciousness or other conditions. That is only one of many possible uses. The following recipes can also be used as part of the preparation and consecration of crystals, skrying tools, pendulums, and other objects. I have also used potions to wash my hands and face before beginning serious work. If you are outdoors, you can use a pitcher filled with a potion to pour a circle around yourself to create a space to work within.

Water is an ingredient in a potion and should be treated as one. Before you heat the water and add the herbs, energize and prepare the water as you would any ingredient. You may wish to put the water outside under the Moon and/or the Sun to absorb their light. A quartz crystal charged and programmed for psychic work can also be placed in the water. When it is time to prepare the potion, heat the water in enamelware, ceramic, glass, cast iron, or stainless steel cookware. Aluminum cookware is problematic for making potions due to chemical and energetic reasons.

Simple Potions

Mexican Tarragon (Mexican Marigold, Dream Marigold)

(Tagetes lucida)

A tablespoon of the leaves and flowers brewed in 12 ounces of hot water for five minutes will do. Strain the mixture and drink it hot or cold. Drinking this potion thirty minutes before psychic work will brighten and strengthen your perceptions. Drink it three nights in a row before retiring for sleep if you are seeking prophetic dreams.

Xhosa Dream Root (African Dream Root)

(Silene capensis or Silene undulata)

First, pound a tablespoon of the root in a mortar and pestle; otherwise, it will have less value. Place the pounded root in 12 ounces of hot water and then beat the solution with a whisk until it is frothy. Let it cool before straining and drinking it. This potion has similar effects and uses to Mexican Marigold, but it is particularly good for astral travel and shamanic work. Drinking it three to five days in a row increases its effect.

Psychic Opener Tea

1 medium bay leaf (crushed)
½ teaspoon cardamom seeds
1 teaspoon damiana
2 teaspoons green tea
1 teaspoon mugwort
1 teaspoon peppermint
½ teaspoon rosemary
1 thread saffron

Use about 1 tablespoon of this mixture per 10 ounces of hot water. Let it brew for at least five minutes, preferably ten minutes. You may add a sweetener if you like, but please use a natural sweetener. The green tea is an active ingredient, so do not leave it out. You begin to feel effects from this tea after thirty minutes, with the effects lasting about three hours.

CHAPTER 15

Chakra Journeys: Pathworkings for the Chakras

Introduction

Working with the chakras is an effective way to encourage spiritual growth and energy perception. If you are unfamiliar with the chakras, think of them as centers of activity in the subtle bodies that are comparable to organs in the physical body. They perform specialized functions in the processing of life energy. I encourage you to look for books and teachers on the topic if it is new to you. Many exercises and techniques to work with the chakras in the bodies of light tend to focus on toning particular sounds, the visualization of colors and symbols, and so on, as their means to accomplish the work. This is a tried-and-true approach, but I've developed another system to work with the chakras. I've written chakra pathworkings to more actively engage the powers of the imagination and also direct perceptions inward to the inner landscape. You may use these even if you are new to chakra work. These pathworkings work on all three levels of the Self but focus most of their impact on the Lower Self. It is the Lower Self, also known as the Dreaming Self or the Primal Self, that is in my estimation the part of Self that must be developed the most if there is to be a deep awareness of the subtle realms.

These pathworkings appear last in this book because the previous exercises, practices, and rituals have prepared you for them. I recommend that you read through the pathworkings several times as a way of implanting the patterns and the images deep into your psyche. Then find a friend to either read them to you or to make recordings of the pathworkings. Although it is not completely necessary, you may also find that these pathworkings are more effective if they are accompanied by a brief ritual. If you do wish to add a ritual to this work, do not make it overly elaborate because that would detract from the impact of the pathworkings themselves. It need only include three essential components: these are the creation of a sacred boundary, a call to your Higher Self, and a declaration of intention for the process. You may design your own ritual, but I have included one here as an example.

Pathworking Ritual

1. Take several deep breaths while imagining the color of a cloudless blue sky. Then hold your cupped hands before you and blow swirling blue energy into your hands. Walk a clockwise circle around the area where you will be doing the pathworking, while marking the air with the blue from your hands. One way to do this is to see one hand as the reservoir and to dip the fingers of the other hand into the blue. When you have come all the way around to where you started, hold up one hand. Blow blue energy onto it, leaving your handprint as a seal hanging in the air or on a convenient surface such as a wall or table.

2. Go to the center of the space and point a finger at a spot a foot above your head. Repeat "By my Light, I call you forth" until you see a radiant star pulsing above your head.
3. Then set the intention of the process. This step may be as simple as making a statement that you are open to being more whole and present in all the realms. It may be that you are aware of specific ways in which you are blocking yourself and wish to name them so that they may be released. Each individual, depending on their circumstances and where they are in their journey, should set their own intention. If you find that after looking inward you are lost for words, look up at the star of your Higher Self and ask for it to set the intention.
4. Proceed now with listening to one of the pathworkings.
5. When you are done with the pathworking, go to the place sealed by your glowing blue handprint. Place your hand on the seal and inhale sharply. This action should release the seal. Now walk counterclockwise and gently disperse the blue boundary, seeing it scatter and fade like mist in the wind.

Using the Pathworkings

I recommend that you start by completing all seven of the pathworkings, starting with the Root Chakra. How often you should do these pathworkings depends on your temperament, your level of training, and your schedule. This actually is strenuous work. One approach is to do one pathworking a week until you complete the set of seven. If you use the pathworking-a-week regimen, plan on taking a break of at least two to three weeks before repeating the series. Another reasonable option is to do a pathworking a day for eight days. After completing the series, wait at least one month before repeating the sequence. During the break, you will continue to receive images, guidance, and remembrances of the pathworkings. If you are inclined to keep a journal of impressions and insights throughout the process, it will help solidify the benefits. After you have completed the full set of pathworkings, you may wish to attempt all of them in one day. When you complete all the pathworkings in one day, the intensity of the effort is counterbalanced by the connections formed by undergoing the whole pattern at once.

If you have already been doing other sorts of chakra work, you may use the pathworking for a specific chakra as a stand-alone exercise to work on a blocked or underdeveloped area. If it is your intention to use these pathworkings as a means to become more aware and more present in the subtle realms, then it is better to work them as a complete set first before going back to address specific weaknesses. If there are also ongoing practices related to the chakras or the subtle bodies, you may continue doing these concurrently with the chakra pathworkings. The chakra pathworkings operate at a different level from most other energetic practices, so there is generally no interference or undesirable interaction, unless you are pushing yourself too hard. Use common sense and listen to your inner wisdom on what is reasonable for you. Beyond that, seek out the guidance of a teacher or a practitioner that you trust. Although I can offer no guarantees that these pathworkings will open your spiritual awareness, I can affirm that they have worked for me and my students.

Note: In the pathworkings presented here, the dots (or ◈◈◈) mean to take a pause, and italics indicate words that need emphasis when the pathworking is read. The number of dots indicates the relative length of the pause.

The Root Chakra Pathworking

Place a hand over your genital area. Take three deep breaths while imagining that your entire body is bathed in red light. Place your body in a comfortable position and close your eyes. Breathe deeply and slowly. If you have any pressing concerns or worries, set them aside. Tell your troubles that you will return to them later but that for now you wish to lay your burdens down. Attend to the sounds around you and any distractions; then dismiss them one by one. Clench your fists tightly for a count of three and then release them. Let all your tension seep away from your body, leaving through your hands.

Close your eyes and see a pearly gray swirling in front of you as if you were inches away from a gauzy curtain ruffled by a breeze. ◈◈◈ You feel a tingle on your face like static electricity. ◈◈◈ Step through the swirling gray. ◈◈◈ Imagine that you are becoming a tree in the midst of a forest. Your feet are sprouting roots that are delving down into the ground. Your roots are slipping through the soil, embracing the ever-larger stones that they find as they dig deeper. Your roots intertwine with the roots of the other plants and trees that surround you. Your roots and the roots of all the trees that you sense around you are digging downward toward the Earth's core. The Earth's core is a fiery ball of molten rock, like a Sun within the Earth, and your roots reach toward it. ◈◈◈◈◈

Now imagine that your arms and hands are boughs and branches reaching upward to the sky. Feel the breezes move through the leaves that are your fingers. ◈◈◈ Now as you stretch upward toward the blazing ball of the Sun, feel the light as it touches your leaves and branches. Feel the other trees reaching skyward with you. Feel the warmth of the Sun on your leaves, your branches, and your boughs. ◈◈◈◈◈

Sense the Sun above you and the fire of the Earth's core below. Find the center of your consciousness, the point that is the seat of your awareness. Let your center of consciousness float free, up and down in your trunk, in your core. Let your consciousness float until it finds a place of stillness and balance between the Sun above and the fire below. ◈◈◈◈

You are the *Tree of your Lives.* ◈◈◈ At the base of the tree lies a powerful serpent; its coils are turning, moving in a slow spiral. What does the serpent look like? ◈◈◈◈◈ Held carefully in its moving coils is a red egg. From glance to glance, the egg changes as it moves in the coils, sometimes brilliant like a ruby and other times a dull, leathery red. Look now into the serpent's eyes and ask it if it has anything to say to you. Listen. ◈◈◈◈◈ Accept the silence or the statement and dwell upon it. ◈◈◈◈◈

The serpent speaks and asks you to enter the red egg. Your center of consciousness leaves the tree and moves down into the center of the red egg. Within the egg, you see every possible shade of red, swirling about you. You see crimson, scarlet, tulip red, cherry red, rose, fire ember red, and many other shades you cannot name. ◈◈◈◈◈ The swirling colors fade away and you can see through the now-crystalline shell of the egg. ◈◈◈◈◈

You look up at the tree and see that it has become Winter. The tree is bare. Snow is heavy upon the boughs, and icicles weigh down the branches. The serpent lies in still, curving loops about the roots. Within the egg, you feel warm and safe at the same time that you are aware of the cold wind that blows outside. ◈◈◈◈◈ The snow and ice begin to melt. Soon all traces of Winter are gone, and the buds begin to swell. Flowers blink open, covering the tree. The flowers' fragrance is faint but distinct. The sunlight has become petals. ◈◈◈◈◈ The flowers fade and fall as leaves unfurl and turn from the light green of spring to the deep green of Summer. New branches grow and twigs spread out to catch the intense warmth of the Sun. Some of the flowers have set and have swollen. ◈◈◈◈◈

The leaves have caught with the fire of Autumn and are ablaze upon the branches. The wind whistles outside, and the crystal egg has chilled. You notice a particular crimson fruit that hangs heavy on the tree. It is egg-shaped and translucent. The fruit is ripe. It falls and is caught in the coils of the serpent. ◈◈◈◈◈

The crystal egg that you are inside of begins to crack and to crumble. The outer shell parts, vanishes, and you are afloat in a red mist.

The mist grows darker, and you sense that you are in motion. ◈◈◈◈◈ The motion stops. The mist clears, and you find that you are now at the center of the fruit that has now become the new egg. The serpent turns its head toward the egg and bids that you depart. You leave the egg and become the tree once again. Your roots dig toward the fire of the Earth, and your branches reach toward the Sun above. ◈◈◈◈◈

Close your eyes and see a pearly gray swirling in front of you as if you were inches away from a gauzy curtain ruffled by a breeze. You feel a tingle on your face like static electricity. ◈◈◈ Step through the swirling gray. ◈◈◈ And you are in the here and the now. You are in your body. You are in the here and the now. Open your eyes slowly. Wiggle your toes and fingers. Breathe deeply. Say your *name* aloud three times.

The Belly Chakra Pathworking

Place your hands on your belly below your navel. Take three deep breaths while imagining that your entire body is bathed in orange light. Place your body in a comfortable position and close your eyes. Breathe deeply and slowly. If you have any pressing concerns or worries, set them aside. Tell your troubles that you will return to them later but that for now you wish to lay your burdens down. Attend to the sounds around you and any distractions; then dismiss them one by one. Clench your fists tightly for a count of three and then release them. Let all your tension seep away from your body, leaving through your hands.

Close your eyes and see a pearly gray swirling in front of you as if you were inches away from a gauzy curtain ruffled by a breeze. You feel a tingle on your face like static electricity. ◈◈◈ Step through the swirling gray. ◈◈◈

You are walking along a shore with the Sun hanging low above the waves to your left. To your right, past the rolling sands, are low cliffs topped with pines. The setting Sun is gilding the trees and painting the cliffs with saffron and ochre. As the warm winds shift back and forth from east to west, you smell the salty sea and the sweet resin of the pines. The back-and-forth of the winds seems to be in time with the sounds of the waves as they break on the shore, giving the impression of long, deep breaths. As you walk the shore, you feel the sand shifting under your feet, giving you a swaying gait. ◈◈◈

Up ahead, the shoreline curves around a place where the cliffs jut toward the sea like a stony jetty. As you get closer to the curve in the cliffs, you hear a soft crackling sound and a softly sighing voice. As you walk the shore, you feel the sand shifting under your feet, giving you a swaying gait. ◈◈◈ You reach the stony cliffs and begin to walk around the bend in the shore. The shore is narrow here so that once every few steps the waves lick at your feet. You come completely around the cliff and see that sands form a wide expanse cradled under the curving arm of the cliffs. In the center of the sands is a roaring bonfire whose *beauty* takes your breath away. The flames leap and dance, swaying in sensuous shapes with the shifting breezes. ◈◈◈ You go to the bonfire and walk around the fire with quick, light steps. Brightly colored shells mark a circle around the bonfire.

Small crabs scurry and skitter around the fire in sideways spirals. ◈◈

The sound of the surf calls your eyes to a shallow tidal pool just beyond the bonfire. That tidal pool is linked to several others looking like huge glass beads reflecting colors of sky and sea and setting Sun. The pools lead to the opening of a cave in the cliffs. You go to get a closer look at the tidal pools. ◈◈◈ You are drawn to walk from pool to pool and toward the cave. ◈◈ You hear the soft sighing of the wind blowing through the mouth of the cave, and it sounds like a voice. You listen to the sounds as you wade into a warm, shallow, tidal pool to approach the cave. You reach the mouth of the cave and feel the urge and enter into the cave. ◈◈

It is dim inside the cave, and you grope in the darkness, feeling the water-smoothed shape of the cave walls. It feels strange yet comforting. Your eyes are slowly adjusting to the dark, but at the same time, the cave is darker the deeper you go.

The passage is narrowing as you journey further inward. You can now feel the walls on both sides of you with your arms outstretched. ◈◈ You take a step, and suddenly you can't touch the walls. The acoustics have changed, and you know that you are in a large chamber. Overcoming a moment of anxiety, you step further into the chamber. ◈◈ The wind and its sighing voice have changed. ◈

The great chamber is growing brighter, and then there is a sun flash. You can see just how large and grand the cavern is. The Sun is setting, and it is at just the right angle for a shaft of light to enter the great chamber. You can see now that there are dozens of stalagmites and stalactites that have grown together to form columns that uphold the chamber. Some of the columns look like fluted tree trunks. Others have curving shapes that remind you of the figures of women and of men, some dancing, some reaching to hold up the ceiling, some alone, and some in full body embraces. The shaft of sunlight is playing off the water in the cave, flinging ribbons and ripples of light across the slippery glossy stones. ◈◈◈

You notice that the light is playing on one of the columns, in particular. A matched pair of stalagmites and stalactites have merged, and there is an incurved hollow whose shape and size are the same as yours. You step closer and carefully examine the colors, shapes, and textures. ◈◈ You step closer, closer, and then press yourself into the hollow. ◈ You feel a rush of sensations and emotions. ◈ Linger in the moment. ◈◈◈◈

The light is growing brighter in the cavern. ◈◈ The warm waters are slowly rising. ◈◈ The light is growing even brighter. ◈◈ You press harder into the cavern's embrace. ◈ The warm waters are slowly rising. ◈◈◈ The sun flash rcaches its peak ◈◈◈ and begins to fade. ◈ You know that it is time to depart. You pull away from the cavern's embrace. ◈ Then you wade out of the great chamber and onto the passage following the fading sunlight. The waters are still rising as the tide comes in. You move toward the mouth of the cave. You can smell the air becoming fresher. ◈

And finally you wade back out through the tidal pool and find yourself on the shore once more.

The waves are lapping at the edge of the bonfire, extinguishing it bit by bit. Only a small sliver of the Sun remains above the horizon. The fringe of a large wave spreads across the bonfire and retreats. The fire is out, but there is still a fiery light at its center. You step closer and see that there is a jewel amidst the blackened remains of the fire. You pick up the jewel and accept its beauty. ◈◈ The wind sighs that it is time to go. ◈◈

Close your eyes and see a pearly gray swirling in front of you as if you were inches away from a gauzy curtain ruffled by a breeze. You feel a tingle on your face like static electricity. ◆◆◆ Step through the swirling gray. ◆◆◆ And you are in the here and the now. You are in your body. You are in the here and the now. Open your eyes slowly. Wiggle your toes and fingers. Breathe deeply. Say your *name* aloud three times.

The Solar Plexus Chakra Pathworking

Place your hands above your navel, but below where your ribs meet. Take three deep breaths while imagining that your entire body is bathed in yellow light. Place your body in a comfortable position and close your eyes. Breathe deeply and slowly. If you have any pressing concerns or worries, set them aside. Tell your troubles that you will return to them later but that for now you wish to lay your burdens down. Attend to the sounds around you and any distractions; then dismiss them one by one. Clench your fists tightly for a count of three and then release them. Let all your tension seep away from your body, leaving through your hands.

Close your eyes and see a pearly gray swirling in front of you as if you were inches away from a gauzy curtain ruffled by a breeze. You feel a tingle on your face like static electricity. ◆◆◆ Step through the swirling gray. ◆◆◆

You are climbing a mountain. ◆◆ The air is crisp and clear with the sharp scent of high, wide-open spaces. The sky is a deep blue, almost cloudless except for thin, lacy traceries of white, far, far aloft. The mountainside is a beautiful patchwork of several shades of green broken up by dark stones that glitter with glints of mica and other minerals. Here and there you see an occasional tree, but you are so high up that the trees are few and far between. ◆◆ As you climb, you peer past the path and see the flat lands and low hills that lie below the mountain. This is the only mountain in this landscape of rich fields, woods, and farmland.

You are climbing with a steady rhythm, taking simple pleasure in the synchrony between the pumping of your legs, your heart, and your breath. ◈◈ Your climb leads you onto a broad rocky shelf on the mountainside. You step onto the shelf and examine it. ◈ You see that three trails lead up the mountain from this place. You study the three trails, trying to decide which one you should take. ◈◈ You listen and look for any clue or sign that might help your choice. ◈◈ One of the trails feels right, so you walk toward it and begin to climb upward again.

Although the air is cool and crisp, you are getting warmer from the effort of the climb. You wipe the sweat from your forehead and dry your hand on your clothing. You climb and climb, the minutes folding into hours. ◈◈◈ The Sun is rising higher in the sky as if it were your companion on this journey. ◈ As you have risen up the mountain and followed its angles and curves, you have come to the realization that it is shaped like an immense dragon with its head turned skyward. You are climbing up its back on a trail that weaves back and forth between its spines. ◈◈◈

Once again, the trail widens and opens onto another rocky shelf, much larger than the first one. You look around, but there does not seem to be any clear trail that leads past this point in the climb. There is a steep stony wall that stretches to the left and to the right. You feel frustrated, but determined to continue. You walk up to the wall and reach out and test the solidity of the many rocks that jut out. It is solid and you decide that it is safe enough to climb the wall. Carefully, you place a foot upon a rock, a hand upon another, and begin to scale the wall. ◈◈ You go up the wall from foothold to foothold with the single-minded strategic focus of a player at a chess tournament. ◈◈◈ Your focus is so tight that you are surprised when you reach the top. ◈ A rush of excitement courses through you as you pull yourself up and stand to survey where you are. To the left and the right, the stony wall sweeps away like two huge wings. ◈ Directly before you are two milky white pillars striped with veins of gold. This surprises you because they are the first objects you've seen on the mountain that look made by human hands. You walk up to them and ◈ you gasp because they stand before a deep chasm, so deep that it is dark even at midday. Your heart falls because you cannot see any way to reach the other side to continue to the summit of the mountain. ◈◈ Frustration, longing, anger, and disappointment swirl within you. To work so hard and be thwarted is intolerable. ◈◈

The two pillars begin to ring with a low, deep sound like harp strings long enough reach to the roots of the mountain. There is a sharp gust of wind, a downdraft, and you look up. High in the sky you see ghostly pillars floating in the sky, wavering as if they were undulating in the wind currents. The deep ringing, thrumming, now comes from the pillars in the sky. The sound is calling you, calling you, drawing your spirit forth. You feel a bit dizzy and drop into a kneeling position. ◈ Your body jerks and then your spirit floats up away from your body toward the sky pillars. ◈◈◈ You reach the airy pillars and see that the Sun is just beyond them. Somehow your ghostly fingers can grasp the pillars, and you launch yourself toward the Sun. ◈◈◈

The ceaseless motion of the Sun's corona casts sparkles into the space around you. You think that you should be feeling heat, but all you feel is zings of electrical energy. You pass through the sparks and fall down into the Sun that now looms so large that you can see nothing else. ◈◈ The Sun's surface is covered with fiery vortices with leaping arcs of liquid light. ◈ You spiral down into a vortex and are dragged down deeper into the Sun. The convection currents roil and turn around you like springs wound from lightning bolts. ◈◈

The motion has stopped; ◈◈ you are at the center of the Sun. ◈◈ Feel the *radiance* streaming forth from you. ◈◈◈ Feel how *you* hold the planets, how *you* hold the center. ◈◈◈◈

Then you are no longer one with the Sun. Once again you feel the tug of the currents, of incandescent star stuff gushing up toward the surface of the Sun. ◈ You feel your speed growing and the pressure building as you streak upward. There is a colossal crashing sound, and you are shot forth from the Sun riding a solar flare. You marvel at the beauty of topaz droplets of the Sun strung on magnetic lines of force carrying you through the blackness of space and back to the blue of Earth's sky. ◈◈

Below you are the airy pillars in the clouds. You fall through them, feeling heavier and denser. You can see your body kneeling before the stony pillars on the mountain. Your descent slows, ◈ slows, ◈◈ and then you gently drop into your body. Feel the shape of your Self. ◈◈◈ You take a deep breath and stand up. You nod your head to honor the pillars and turn to begin your descent down the mountain. The plateau has changed. There is a golden boulder with a flattened top in the center of the plateau. You go and sit upon the boulder, and feel the wholeness of your journey. ◈◈◈◈ Now it is time to depart.

Close your eyes and see a pearly gray swirling in front of you as if you were inches away from a gauzy curtain ruffled by a breeze. You feel a tingle on your face like static electricity. ◈◈◈ Step through the swirling gray. ◈◈◈ And you are in the here and the now. You are in your body. You are in the here and the now. Open your eyes slowly. Wiggle your toes and fingers. Breathe deeply. Say your *name* aloud three times.

The Heart Chakra Pathworking

Place your hands on the center of your chest, between your breasts. Take three deep breaths while imagining that your entire body is bathed in green light. Place your body in a comfortable position and close your eyes. Breathe deeply and slowly. If you have any pressing concerns or worries, set them aside. Tell your troubles that you will return to them later but that for now you wish to lay your burdens down. Attend to the sounds around you and any distractions; then dismiss them one by one. Clench your fists tightly for a count of three and then release them. Let all your tension seep away from your body, leaving through your hands.

Close your eyes and see a pearly gray swirling in front of you as if you were inches away from a gauzy curtain ruffled by a breeze. You feel a tingle on your face like static electricity. ◈◈◈ Step through the swirling gray. ◈◈◈

Cold is the night and dry the oak leaves that rattle and whisper in the driving snow. ◈ You wrap your cloak tighter around you as the wind's cold fingers try to pry it from you. It is hard trudging through the snow-packed trail, and you are grateful for your boots and for the trail that many travelers have carved through the forest. You listen to the sounds of the forest at night as you walk. The bare boughs and branches of the forest canopy seem to just barely hold up the sky of leaden clouds. ◈◈ It looks a bit brighter ahead, and you hope that there is a clearing where you might pause to rest and perhaps build a fire. ◈◈

You push past a low-hanging spruce branch and see a snow-covered field dotted with the stubble of last season's harvest. ◈ At the end of the field, you see a castle, lights aglow, and the scent of wood smoke on the air. ◈◈ Your heart lifts, and you run through the field to the castle's great door. ◈◈

The door is tall enough and broad enough so that a rider could enter astride a horse. The ironwork is done in an intricate leafy design. There is a hefty door knocker in the shape of a face. You study it ◈◈ and then knock three times. ◈◈◈ The door creaks open, and you are dazzled by the light; the sound of music, laughter, and voices comes spilling forth. A big burly doorman says, "Greetings and welcome, traveler!" but then he looks straight through you ◈ and has a quizzical expression on his face. You speak but he does not hear you. He shrugs and begins to close the door, so you rush past him into the castle. It seems that you are *invisible.* •

You take a deep breath of the warm, moist air filled with the spicy scents of food and drink and sweet smoke. The castle is filled with people dancing, singing, cavorting, dressed in outlandish Winter festival garb. ◈ Rich green velvets, swags of vines, feathers, beads, and candelabras adorn the many well-appointed halls. A group of revelers comes your way, and you swerve to avoid jostling against them. You are invisible to them as well. ◈ In swerving, you find that you are more than invisible, you are insubstantial—for you have walked through a fully laden banquet table. ◈ This troubles you but also delights you because you can move through the throng and see whatever you like without hindrance. You go exploring. ◈◈◈

After a time, you are no longer content to just look at the dancers, the jugglers, the lovers embracing; no longer content to listen to the storytellers, or to stand with an empty plate before the feast. This joyful celebration, this respite from the cold night, now seems hollow. You look around to find a place to rest and to think. ◈◈ At the end of a ballroom, you see a beautiful, colossal hearth carved from jade. A small, inviting fire burns within it. You go to the jade hearth to warm yourself. On the mantle there is a jade loving cup adorned with swans. It is a stunning piece of art and craft, and you reach out to touch it. To your great surprise and relief, you find that you can pick it up. As soon as you pick it up, the figures of a naked woman and a naked man step forth from the flames. They look so similar that were it not for their genders, you would think them twins. ◈◈

They look at you; they can see you! They tell you to drink of the mead of poetry. You give them a puzzled look, and they point to the cup in your hands. You bring the cup to your lips, smelling the rich, honey, floral aroma and drink. The mead has been warmed by the hearth, and you can feel warmth spreading through you with each sip. ◈◈ You offer the cup to the twins, and with a smile, they each take a sip and place the loving cup back onto the jade hearth. They come up to you and, each taking one of your hands, guide you to a small altar next to the hearth. On the altar you see rattles, drums, chimes, pipes, and other instruments. They tell you to choose one. ◈◈◈ You make your selection and they kiss you. Then they bow to you and walk into the flames of the hearth and dissolve back into them. ◈◈

Revelers are gathering in a circle in the ballroom. The drummers and musicians have all gathered, and with the music come the dancers. A few stragglers have just entered from the hallway, and one of them links arms with you and drags you along. You can be seen by all. The time of celebration has come. You join in with your instrument, your voice, and dance along in the circle. ◈◈◈◈

The night has passed in merriment, and the time for departures has come. The burly doorman who let you into the castle notices you and asks if you were the one who came late. You answer "Yes" and he takes a green cloak off a peg and places it on your shoulders. In groups of two and three, revelers come up to you, and they affix jewelry, ribbons, bells, and shells to the gifting cloak. ◈◈◈ When they are done, you offer heartfelt thanks. ◈◈ With an arm across your shoulder, the doorman takes you to the great door with the leafy ironwork. He opens the door, and you depart on your journey. ♦

Close your eyes and see a pearly gray swirling in front of you as if you were inches away from a gauzy curtain ruffled by a breeze. You feel a tingle on your face like static electricity. ♦♦♦ Step through the swirling gray. ♦♦♦ And you are in the here and the now. You are in your body. You are in the here and the now. Open your eyes slowly. Wiggle your toes and fingers. Breathe deeply. Say your *name* aloud three times.

The Throat Chakra Pathworking

Place your hands on your throat. Take three deep breaths while imagining that your entire body is bathed in sky-blue light. Place your body in a comfortable position and close your eyes. Breathe deeply and slowly. If you have any pressing concerns or worries, set them aside. Tell your troubles that you will return to them later but that for now you wish to lay your burdens down. Attend to the sounds around you and any distractions you have noted; then dismiss them one by one. Clench your fists tightly for a count of three and then release them. Let all your tension seep away from your body, leaving through your hands.

Close your eyes and see a pearly gray swirling in front of you as if you were inches away from a gauzy curtain ruffled by a breeze. You feel a tingle on your face like static electricity. ♦♦♦ Step through the swirling gray. ♦♦♦

The full Moon hangs high overhead, surrounded by three pale rings of blue. To the east, you see strips of dark clouds racing in your direction. ♦♦ You hear a faint raucous sound that quickly becomes louder and identifiable as birds. You can see now that the clouds are not clouds but rivers of birds. ♦♦ They grow louder and fill the sky above you as they dash over you on some unknown errand of great urgency. The quiet that follows is profound. ◈◈ You listen carefully to make sure that you have not been struck deaf by the torrent of birds. ◈◈◈

The ground begins to shake, and you hear a vibration so deep that the marrow in your bones quivers. The ground pitches and shakes so hard that you fall down on all fours. Your mouth tastes of metal, and your heart is pounding loudly but not loudly enough to cover the sound of stone snapping and wrenching. ◈ All around you, slabs of stone are pushing up through the soil, forming a stone circle with you as its center. ◈◈◈ As quickly as this tempest came, it ceases. You struggle to your feet and look at the circle of stones. Atop each stone there is a flute, a chime, or a harp made of gems and silver. A translucent blue fire dances on each stone; ◈◈ sporadically the blue fire leaps from stone to stone. You look more closely and see that each stone is covered in symbols, runes, and glyphs that vanish and appear with the brightening and the dimming of the blue fire. They seem to come from many different languages and cultures. ◈◈ You walk around the circle examining each one. ◈◈◈

With each step, it feels as if the air is getting thicker. ◈◈ You return to the center of the circle. There is a magnetic pull that is holding you, placing you in the center of the circle. ◈◈ There is a brief pulse of light like heat lightning. ◈ It happens again. ◈ You look up and the Moon is pulsing with light. As it pulses, it flings off hoops of brilliance. ◈◈ The Moon is directly over you, and with each pulse, the Moon drops lower and lower. ◈◈◈ A thick mantle of power, of presence, of the Divine hangs over the stone circle. •• The hairs rise on your arms, and a cold shiver runs up your spine. ◈◈ You know that you are in the presence of one of the Great Ones. ◈◈ You experience the awe and panic of feeling the tingling breath of the Divine upon you. ◈◈◈

A voice so filled with the tones of music that it can scarcely be called a voice says, "Child and Apprentice, I am that who gave you the Breath and the Mystery. Child and Apprentice, who owns your words and who owns your voice? Tell me truly; I grow melancholy for lack of your voice." ◈◈◈ You know that you should answer, but you do not know what or how to say it. ◈◈ The silence grows deep and long as the light continues to pulse. ◈◈ You begin to form an answer, but when you open your mouth, nothing comes out. ◈◈◈

The great voice rumbles now with the sound of tumbling boulders and waterfalls.

"I have given you this circle of words and sounds and symbols . . . is that not enough?"

You try again, but now you can find neither your thoughts nor your words. ◈◈ There is a great pulse of light, and a wand and a dagger float in the air before you. Somehow you know that you should take one. ◈ You choose one and feel a rush of power in your hand. At that moment, the flutes, chimes, and harps of the stone circle all call out. ◈◈ The circle is your orchestra, and the tool in your hand your baton. You pour your memories, your hopes, your fears, your understanding of your life into the circle, brandishing your tool and making the circle tell your story. ◈◈ The music is indescribable, and the blue fire takes the shape of every thought and feeling. ◈◈◈◈

You falter for a moment, thinking that you have expressed all that you have, but then more comes spilling out. ◈◈◈ Finally, you bring the last thing forth that you wish to convey at this time, and the circle goes quiet. ◈◈ The Divine presence feels lighter, and you can hear crickets and the familiar sounds of the night. You feel a tingling brush against your face and find a single tear. The voice says, "My thanks for your effort; it is *all* I can ask of you." ◈◈ You manage to whisper, "Thank you." Your voice has returned, and the tool in your hand remains as a reminder and a blessing. ◈◈

The Moon is rising, rising back to its celestial home. ◈◈◈ The stones are wrapped in veils of blue fire that are growing paler. The stone circle is vanishing like windblown mist, and soon no trace of it will remain. ◈◈ In the distance, you can hear the sound of the rivers of birds. ◈◈◈

Close your eyes and see a pearly gray swirling in front of you as if you were inches away from a gauzy curtain ruffled by a breeze. You feel a tingle on your face like static electricity. ◈◈◈ Step through the swirling gray. ◈◈◈ And you are in the here and the now. You are in your body. You are in the here and the now. Open your eyes slowly. Wiggle your toes and fingers. Breathe deeply. Say your *name* aloud three times.

The Brow Chakra Pathworking

Place your hands on your forehead. Take three deep breaths while imagining that your entire body is bathed in deep indigo light. Place your body in a comfortable position and close your eyes. Breathe deeply and slowly. If you have any pressing concerns or worries, set them aside. Tell your troubles that you will return to them later but that for now you wish to lay your burdens down. Attend to the sounds around you and any distractions; then dismiss them one by one. Clench your fists tightly for a count of three and then release them. Let all your tension seep away from your body, leaving through your hands.

Close your eyes and see a pearly gray swirling in front of you as if you were inches away from a gauzy curtain ruffled by a breeze. You feel a tingle on your face like static electricity. ◈◈◈ Step through the swirling gray. ◈◈◈

You are in the desert, and sand stretches for as far as the eye can see. The light has an odd quality to it that you can't define. ◈◈ You look down at the sand, and you see that you have four shadows. You look up and turn on your heel and see that there are four Suns hanging low near the horizon. The cloudless sky above is an opulent indigo hue. It is neither hot nor cold, and you cannot tell if it is dawn or dusk. ◈◈ You have no idea where the compass points might be, but the Suns are equally spaced around you. ◈◈ You begin to feel a quivering in the soles of your feet. It feels like a current is building in the Earth deep beneath you. The current rises into your legs. ◈ The charge is rising in your thighs. ◈ The tingle is rising up your torso. ◈ The charge is rising in your neck. ◈ The power rises and stops in your forehead. ◈◈ You see the image of a pyramid in your mind's eye, and you know that you must build it.

You lift up your hands, palms upraised, and feel the tingling grow upon your brow. ◈ Course by course, the stones are being laid, building the four walls of a pyramid around you. ◈ The walls are rising, and with them, the light of the four Suns is diminishing. ◈ The walls are rising, and with them, the light of the four Suns is diminishing, and what light remains is mixed with the deep indigo of the sky above. ◈ Finally, the capstone is placed, and you are in a profound darkness. • It is silent, and the only thing that you hear is the beating of your heart amplified by the walls of the pyramid. ◈◈◈

Then one by one stars begin to appear in the vast blackness. ◈ Faint points of light, stars so large that they sparkle with the fire of gems, and luminous filigrees of nebulae appear before you. ◈ You float in the heavens adrift, standing on a square of onyx. ◈◈ You inhale and find that you can breathe the thin ether of space. You feel a tug, and you know that you are accelerating. The stars are moving past you. You do not know where you are going, but it is enough to know where you have been and where this will lead. ◈◈ You observe that some stars are dimming and going out, remaining as cinders, while other stars flare into being, still swaddled in the clouds of their birth. You are traveling in time as well as space. ◈◈

You hear a sound that you can just make out at the extreme range of your hearing. It sounds like an aria so high that it seems sung by hummingbirds and a play of tones so sonorous that it sounds like French horns large enough for the hands of giants. ◈◈ The sound seems to follow the changes in the stars. ◈ Then a ripple passes through all of space as if an unseen pebble had been dropped into space. You look around to find the cause of this ripple but see nothing. ◈ You look more carefully. ◈ Still nothing. ◈ You focus yourself and look again. This time you see a huge outline in the darkness, like a shape cut from glass sliding across velvet. ◈ The outline is coming toward you, and as it does, it becomes smaller and takes on the form of a Goddess. ◈◈

She is hovering above you now, a cloaked figure wrapped in the jet of space, spangled with stars. A sweet fragrance fills the air. ◈ She has come to tell you something—listen. ◈◈◈◈◈ And listen again. ◈◈◈ You offer her thanks for what she has shared. ◈◈ She throws back her cloak and smiles upon you. ◈ Next, she stretches forth her hands and with a turn of her wrists causes a circular firepit to appear on the onyx floor before you. She plucks a star from her brow and places it in the firepit. An ethereal violet flame springs up in the firepit. ◈ For the briefest of instants, she looks you in the eye, and your blood chills with the grandeur and the mystery that burns within her. ◈ She beckons you to step into the flame. ◈

You place a foot upon the hearth. ◈ By force of will and trust, you step into the flame. ◈ You feel both hot and cold, wet and dry, and your body begins to become as clear as crystal. ◈ Rather than dancing around you, the violet flame passes through you, into you, illuminating you. ◆◆ You feel an incredible pressure building in the center of your forehead. The flames are concentrating there. ◆◆ It is becoming so bright that you try to clench your eyes shut, but your lids are as transparent as the rest of you. ◆◆ You think that you can bear no more, and without warning, a Third Eye opens upon your brow and the flames rush out through it. ◆◆◆

You can *see*. You can see the desert and the pyramid. You can see the rings of Saturn. You can see the first lake you ever saw. You can see your first love. You can see everywhere and everywhen. ◆◆◆ You see yourself. ◆ You hear her voice say, "Come back to me!" The flames go out. She has wrapped you inside her cloak of night. You hear again the aria so high it seems sung by hummingbirds and a play of tones so sonorous that it sounds like French horns large enough for the hands of giants. The Third Eye on your forehead slowly closes. She is sending you home.

Close your two eyes and see a pearly gray swirling in front of you as if you were inches away from a gauzy curtain ruffled by a breeze. You feel a tingle on your face like static electricity. ◆◆◆ Step through the swirling gray. ◆◆◆ And you are in the here and the now. You are in your body. You are in the here and the now. Open your eyes slowly. Wiggle your toes and fingers. Breathe deeply. Say your *name* aloud three times.

The Crown Chakra Pathworking

Hold your hands on the top of your head over the spot that was the soft circle when you were an infant. Take three deep breaths while imagining that your entire body is bathed in violet light.

Place your body in a comfortable position and close your eyes. Breathe deeply and slowly. If you have any pressing concerns or worries, set them aside. Tell your troubles that you will return to them later but that for now you wish to lay your burdens down. Attend to the sounds around you and any distractions; then dismiss them one by one. Clench your fists tightly for a count of three and then release them. Let all your tension seep away from your body, leaving through your hands.

Close your eyes and see a pearly gray swirling in front of you as if you were inches away from a gauzy curtain ruffled by a breeze. You feel a tingle on your face like static electricity. ◆◆◆ Step through the swirling gray. ◆◆◆

You are walking slowly through a tunnel of glowing crystals. ◆ The walls are pulsing with moving bands of light that lead you onward. ◆◆ The crystals shine brighter and with a burst of light, all the colors dissolve into rotating bands of clouds and winds as if the sky had been rolled into a tube. ◆◆ You are walking a bit faster now. ◆◆ With a sweeping, churning motion, the tunnel changes from sky to sea. ◆ The ripples of light are moving you onward faster. ◆◆ You can no longer walk; you are being carried along by the flow. ◆◆ The vortex of waters begins to froth and glow brighter. ◆◆ Sparks grow brighter and larger, and turn by turn, the waters become curling flames of purple. You are flying faster and faster through the tunnel of flames. ◆◆ You reach the end of the tunnel and shoot out, passing through a light so bright that you can see no details. ◆◆

White with opalescent hints of color is all that you can see in front of you, above you, below you, to the left, to the right, and behind you. ◆ You become aware that you are seeing in all directions at once without movement. ◆◆ There is a sense of calm that hovers in this place. ◆ You float like a shimmer in an opal, motionless, still but shifting with the light. ◆◆◆ You are a point of consciousness. ◆ You are a point of brilliance. ◆◆

A translucent outline in the shape of your body forms around your brilliant point of consciousness. ◆◆ Another translucent outline in the shape of your body, larger than the first, forms around your brilliant point of consciousness. ◈◈ A vibration beyond sound fills your being. ◈ A third outline forms around your center of consciousness. ◈◈ A fourth, less-distinct outline forms around your center of consciousness. ◈◈◈ A glowing oval forms around the concentric sheaths of energy. ◈◈

You feel yourself expanding. ◈◈◈ You feel yourself expanding. ◈◈ You feel yourself expanding. ◈

You become aware that the glowing white opalescence surrounding you is not as featureless as it first appeared. As you open yourself to perceive more, you sense thoughts, emotions, images flowing around and through you. ◈ You sense the essences of beings like yourself, beings smaller than you, and beings so huge as to be almost unimaginable. ◈◈ Moment by moment you are becoming aware of more and more of the *web* and the *weave* of consciousness that is the Universe. ◈◈ Wave fronts of various shapes and sizes are coming from all directions. Some pass through each other unchanged, and others interact in many ways, changing and producing new waves and vibrations. ◈◈ Some parts of these mercurial patterns hint at meanings, and there are more and more the longer you look. ◈◈ It is not chaotic; it is just more than you can grasp, though there are infinitesimal moments when you see the outline of the All. ◈◈ It is not exactly like breathing, but you become cognizant of an influx and an outflow of light. ◈◈ You focus on the simple, slow rhythm of in and out, ◈ in and out. ◈◈

There is no rhythm now, only the sense of a constant circular motion. One of the patterns, one of the wave fronts, has concentrated itself into a single dot. ◈ You look at the dot, and as you focus your attention on it, your vision zooms in until you see that it is a circle, not a point. ◈◈ Your eyes detect motion: the circle is spinning. You focus on its center and see a small point there. ◈ You look at a bright point, and as you focus on it, once again your vision zooms in and you see that it is a circle, not a point. ◈ From point to circle, ◈ from point to circle, you ride the circuit of the infinite small and the infinite large. ◈◈◈◈ There is no rhythm now, only the sense of a constant motion, which is stillness of a sort. ◈◈ Silence ◈ Stillness ◈ Wholeness ◈◈◈

Then the web and weave of wave fronts of various shapes and sizes coming from all directions become distinct. Some pass through each other unchanged, and others interact in many ways, changing and producing new waves and vibrations. ◈◈ The wave fronts coalesce into the opaline brightness. There, projected on the all-pervasive whiteness, you see a *vision*. ◈◈◈◈◈

Then you are being carried along in the tunnel of flames. ◈ You are flying faster and faster through the tunnel of flames. ◈◈ The flames shorten to sparks that begin to dim. ◈

Turn by turn the flames curl and then swirl into a vortex of rippling waters. ◈◈ With a sweeping, churning motion, the tunnel changes from sea to sky. You pass by rotating bands of clouds and wind as if the sky had been rolled into a tube. ◈◈ You are traveling more slowly now, and your feet touch down. You are walking in the tunnel. ◈ The clouds are becoming chunky and sharp edged, and they morph into glowing crystals. ◈ You are walking slowly through a tunnel of glowing crystals. ◈ The walls are pulsing with moving bands of light that lead you outward. ◈ You are out. ◈◈

Close your eyes and see a pearly gray swirling in front of you as if you were inches away from a gauzy curtain ruffled by a breeze. You feel a tingle on your face like static electricity. ◈◈◈ Step through the swirling gray. ◈◈◈ And you are in the here and the now. You are in your body. You are in the here and the now. Open your eyes slowly. Wiggle your toes and fingers. Breathe deeply. Say your *name* aloud three times.

CHAPTER 16

Closing Thoughts

The more you work with your psychic senses, the more you are likely to trust them. The more you trust in their accuracy and utility, the more they will unfold and develop. This is a natural cycle, but it does need nurturing, protection, and sometimes a reset. Somewhat paradoxically, doubting enough to test your psychic perceptions regularly leads to trusting them more. Whenever you can, see if an external and ideally objective source of information confirms, partially confirms, or refutes your psychic perceptions. This will allow you to see how you need to adjust your aim to hit the mark more frequently.

Confirming your psychic perceptions will always be a balancing act, as you walk the line between conviction in your perceptions and the possibility that your perceptions are fantasies. Imagine the quandary that a hurricane forecaster must have. The science and craft of weather prediction are far from perfect even with the best data, models, and the experience of a skilled forecaster. However, the moment comes that a prediction must be made and a warning issued. There are consequences to being right, being wrong, and all the shades in between. Even if the situation is not as dire as a hurricane, there are still consequences. When information that comes from psychism has an impact on your words, deeds, or feelings, it is changing the course of your life by some number of degrees. When you give counsel and information to others, you have the potential of altering their course as well.

Harkening back to the beginning of this book, with the development of skills also comes a need to develop your integrity, ethics, and duty. In the early stages of your development, this keeps you from shutting yourself down. In the later stages of your development, this is what helps maintain your emotional and mental health. Using your psychism can be a source of strength and pride, or it can be a drain and a source of soul-corroding drama.

When you have the keys to opening the doors to a more expansive reality, the universe is both brighter and darker. Beauty has always been in the eye of the beholder, so the more you see, the more it behooves you to seek beauty. As you can hear more of what the Universe is saying, it is valuable to think of it as poetry that contains many levels and meanings. As you reach out to touch farther than you can reach with your physical hands, ask yourself if you are offering kindness, healing, and guidance. The more present you are in this expanded reality, the more it is present in you. When you become aware of more and more frequencies and types of energy and spirit, you may realize that there is no place that is not lit and filled with the presence of life in all its forms. The shadows are just the places where the light is being absorbed, blocked, or reflected by the manifestation of those forms. When your senses adjust, you'll see that the darkness also glows with its own sort of radiance, and the cycle of extending and refining your perception starts again.

Lest you think this is all a serious and somber matter, I'll remind you that opening your subtle senses can also lead to playful delight and wonder in the world that surrounds you. Often it will be the joy of exploration and discovery that will lead you onward. You may also discover the thrill that comes when you help others in their journeys as well. You have the keys; now the rest is up to you.

Recommended Reading

Ashcroft-Nowicki, Dolores. *Highways of the Mind: The Art and History of Pathworking.* Sechelt, British Columbia: Twin Eagles Publishing, 2011. ISBN-13: 978-1896238104.

Biffle, Christopher. *The Castle of the Pearl.* New York: HarperCollins, 1990. ISBN-13: 978-0060965068.

Dominguez Jr., Ivo. *Casting Sacred Space: The Core of All Magickal Work.* San Francisco: Weiser Books, 2012. ISBN-13: 978-1578634996.

Dominguez Jr., Ivo. *Spirit Speak: Knowing and Understanding Spirit Guides, Ancestors, Ghosts, Angels, and the Divine.* Wayne, NJ: New Page Books, 2008. ISBN-13: 978-1601630025.

Eason, Cassandra. *The Complete Crystal Bible: 500 Crystals to Heal Your Body, Mind and Spirit.* London: Carlton Books Ltd., 2015. ISBN-13: 978-1780976297.

Harrison, Karen. *The Herbal Alchemist's Handbook: A Grimoire of Philtres, Elixirs, Oils, Incense, and Formulas for Ritual Use.* San Francisco: Weiser Books, 2011. ISBN-13: 978-1578634910.

Hope, Murry. *Practical Techniques of Psychic Self-Defense.* New York: St. Martin's Press, 1986. ISBN-13: 978-0312635527.

Penczak, Christopher. *The Mystic Foundation: Understanding and Exploring the Magical Universe.* St. Paul, MN: Llewellyn Publications, 2006. ISBN-13: 978-0738709796.

Pond, David. *Chakras for Beginners: A Guide to Balancing Your Chakra Energies.* St. Paul, MN: Llewellyn Publications, 1999. ISBN-13: 978-1567185379.

Regardie, Israel. *The Middle Pillar: The Balance between Mind and Magic.* St. Paul, MN: Llewellyn Publications, 2002. ISBN-13: 978-1567181401.

Smith, Jacki, and Patty Shaw. *Do It Yourself Akashic Wisdom: Access the Library of Your Soul.* San Francisco: Weiser Books, 2013. ISBN-13: 978-1578635405.

Wildman, Laura. *Wiccan Meditations: The Witch's Way to Personal Transformation.* New York: Citadel, 2002. ISBN-13: 978-0806523460.

About the Author

Andreanna Pharis

Ivo Dominguez Jr. is a visionary and practitioner of a variety of esoteric disciplines. He was a founding member of Keepers of the Holly Chalice, the first coven of the Assembly of the Sacred, a Wiccan syncretic tradition that draws inspiration from astrology, Qabalah, the Western Magickal Tradition, and the folk religions of Europe. A professional astrologer, Ivo has studied astrology since 1980. Visit him at *www.ivodominguezjr.com*.

About the Author

To Our Readers

Weiser Books, an imprint of Red Wheel/Weiser, publishes books across the entire spectrum of occult, esoteric, speculative, and New Age subjects. Our mission is to publish quality books that will make a difference in people's lives without advocating any one particular path or field of study. We value the integrity, originality, and depth of knowledge of our authors.

Our readers are our most important resource, and we appreciate your input, suggestions, and ideas about what you would like to see published.

Visit our website at *www.redwheelweiser.com* to learn about our upcoming books and free downloads, and be sure to go to *www.redwheelweiser.com/newsletter* to sign up for newsletters and exclusive offers.

You can also contact us at *info@rwwbooks.com* or at

Red Wheel/Weiser, LLC
65 Parker Street, Suite 7
Newburyport, MA 01950